Grilling & Barbecuing

FOOD AND FIRE IN REGIONAL AMERICAN COOKING

Denis Kelly

PHOTOGRAPHS BY
Maren Caruso

STEWART, TABORI & CHANG • NEW YORK

To my wife, Kathryn

Published in 2003 by
Stewart, Tabori & Chang
A Company of La Martinière Groupe
115 West 18th Street
New York, NY 10011

Export Sales to all countries except
Canada, France, and French-speaking Switzerland:
Thames and Hudson Ltd.
181A High Holborn
London WC1V 7QX
England

Canadian Distribution:
Canadian Manda Group
One Atlantic Avenue, Suite 105
Toronto, Ontario M6K 3E7
Canada

Library of Congress Cataloging-in-Publication Data
Kelly, Denis, 1939-
    Grilling & barbecuing: food and fire in regional American cooking/Denis Kelly ; photographs by Maren Caruso.
        p. cm.
    Includes bibliographical references and index.
    ISBN 1-58479-237-X
        1. Barbecue cookery. I. Title: Grilling and barbecuing. II. Title.

TX840.B3 K4397 2003
641.5'784--dc21

20022042798

Additional photo credits:
p. 89 © Digital Vision; p. 93 © EyeWire; p. 97 © PhotoDisc (photograph: Mitch Hrdlicka); p. 116 © PhotoDisc (photograph: Ryan McVay); p. 151 © Digital Vision; p. 157 © PhotoDisc

PRINTED IN SINGAPORE

10 9 8 7 6 5 4 3 2 1

FIRST PRINTING

Contents

| Preface: Food and Fire | 8 |

| Grilling and Barbecuing: An American Way of Cooking | 11 |

| Grilling Techniques and Equipment | 34 |

| Ingredients | 54 |

| Fish & Seafood | 63 |

| Birds | 83 |

| Pork | 109 |

| Beef | 135 |

| Lamb | 161 |

| Vegetables & Fruit | 175 |

| Sources | 200 |

| Index | 202 |

Preface: Food and Fire

I grew up burning my fingers on food hot from the grill. I'd stand in the smoke near the backyard barbecue when my dad was grilling the Sunday burgers or chickens or steaks, and he'd use me for quality control, slipping me a corner of the steak or a bit of burger or a chicken wing, and asking, "Done yet?" I'd transfer the hot bit from my fingers to my mouth, whistle in some air to cool it down, mumble, "Tastes good to me!" and another summer dinner would be ready. This ritual, enacted again and again as I grew up, seems to me now to define my childhood, and perhaps a part of our lives that can be called distinctly American.

There is something about that backyard barbecue that defines a way of life. Sure, it's only cooking, and I know that they like to cook food on the grill in other countries, but in America we've taken this type of outdoor cooking and made it into our own special way of preparing food and celebrating the values of family, neighbors, and home. Whether it's a simple charcoal grill on the patio or a gas barbecue on the back deck or a built-in barbecue pit big enough to roast a shoat in, there's a way of life in America that centers around an outdoor hearth, a place where fire and food and family come together in rituals that seem to define us.

In this book I'll search out and describe these rituals and see how each region of the country has its own way of putting food and fire together. We'll learn how grilling and hearth cookery were the original way of cooking in colonial America and how barbecuing, originally an American Indian method of grilling meats and fish, spread out from the South to become one of the most popular types of cooking in the country today.

I'll provide recipes for regional specialties such as the smoky long-cooked pork barbecue in the South and savory pit-roasted beef in Texas, grilled fish and seafood on the coasts, chile-laced meats, poultry, and vegetables on the grill in the Southwest, and the classic backyard favorites of juicy steaks, savory chicken, and grilled hamburgers with the works. Recipes from all of America's regional grilling and barbecuing traditions will be found in chapters on seafood and fish, birds, pork, beef, lamb, and vegetables and fruit. I'll tell you how to build and prepare charcoal, hardwood, and gas fires in every type of grill available today and how to grill, roast, or barbecue a wide variety of delicious foods. Ingredients and equipment will be explained and sources provided for hard-to-find foods, grills, and tools. You'll have all you need to become proficient at the quintessential American ways of cooking: grilling and barbecuing.

Grilling and Barbecuing: An American Way of Cooking

Most of us in the United States have grown up eating food cooked outdoors over fire. Whether it's hamburger seared and smoking from a backyard barbecue, steak and corn on the cob grilled over coals, or smoky long-cooked pork ribs in a spicy sauce, grilled or barbecued food seems to define American cookery. In every region of the country, whether you grew up in Secaucus or Seattle, Memphis or Monterey, you'll find food that's cooked over the fire in the open air. And you'll often get into an argument about it.

Like baseball and politics, grilling and barbecuing in America are definitely local. And, like baseball and politics, Americans are not shy about defending the home-town point of view. Mention the word barbecue to someone from Texas and you'll get some strong opinions: It's beef brisket, smoky and long-cooked, but some like their beef basted with a chile-laced sauce with beans on the side and others prefer it with just salt and pepper and served on a piece of butcher paper. Folks from Memphis will have other opinions: Here they'll be boasting about their pit-smoked spareribs, but some will ask for their ribs "dry" with a spicy rub, and others swear by "wet" ribs bathed in a sweet and tangy tomato sauce. In North Carolina they'll insist on a vinegary pepper sauce mopped on the whole hog, while South Carolinians will call for a mustard-based sauce on their pulled pork shoulder. These might not be a very important questions to many of us, but they sure matter in Texas, Memphis, and the Carolinas.

And if you head north or east or west to anywhere above the line that Mr. Mason and Mr. Dixon drew all those years ago, you'll get other answers. Barbecue is what Dad does on the patio every summer Sunday with sauce-brushed chicken sputtering on the grill, clouds of smoke swirling around him, cold beer in hand and a few more in the cooler. Or it's what happens to salmon when it's hot-smoked over alder fires on the shores of Puget Sound in the Pacific Northwest. Or what the grill man does in So Cal with shark steaks sprinkled with chile and lime and served in a taco with salsa fresca. Food on the fire, by whatever word you choose to describe it, whether you call it grilling or barbecuing, is the American way of cooking.

Whatever region you come from and whatever techniques and ingredients you passionately defend, you are part of an American tradition of cooking that goes back to the origins of our culture. While cooking itself begins with grilling over fire,

Americans have adopted a distinctive style of grill cookery as their own. Certainly other cultures grill food upon occasion: Provençal lamb *grillé au feu du bois*, Tuscan *bistecca à la fiorentina*, and Greek *souvlaki* are a few dishes that come to mind. But in America we have created a type of grill cooking that reflects a way of life based on an outdoor lifestyle, access to plenty of meat and fresh vegetables, and a casual approach to preparing and eating our food. The backyard barbecue tells us more about who we are than any formal multicourse meal in a fancy restaurant could ever do.

Food and Fire: A Short History

Fire makes us human. Sometime in the distant past (some say 500,000 years ago, others push the date back even further) our ancestors created the hearth, the campfire, a source of warmth and protection that nurtured the social bonds that make up our humanity. Bringing fire into the center of our lives also gave us the power to transform what we took from the natural world—meat, vegetables, roots, seeds—into food that helped to change inarticulate hominids roaming the savannahs to fully human members of complex societies. Claude Lévi-Strauss, the French anthropologist, calls this the transition from the raw to the cooked, from nature to culture.

Cooking is basic to human life and to the development of society. When meat is cooked, Harold McGee tells us in *On Food and Cooking: Science and Lore of the Kitchen*, four things occur: We make the meat safe to eat by destroying harmful bacteria; we break down tough fibers and muscles and the meat becomes easier to chew; we can better digest and assimilate the denatured proteins in the meat; and, perhaps most important, we make meat more flavorful. Many vegetables, seeds, and tubers become palatable only through cooking, and some poisonous plants (manioc, for example) become edible only through heating and processing.

Some anthropologists feel that the nutritional breakthroughs brought about by cooking provided the access to protein that resulted in the evolutionary leap from proto-human hominids to fully human *Homo erectus*. Fossil evidence shows us that a larger brain and the resulting tool-making ability coincide with a change in tooth structure that indicates a switch to meat eating; the presence of fire is indicated by hearths that date back to the emergence of the species. And archaeologists tell us that cave dwellings of Peking man from half a million years ago and remains of campfires in southern Europe dating from the same period show evidence of grilling and roasting meat.

But there is also an aspect to cooking that is more than simply nutritional. Cooking and sharing food around the campfire involves complex social interactions that nurture and require symbolic activity and create culture. Lévi-Strauss sees food preparation and allocation as a way of thinking about who we are and how we relate to each other. Our food, our way of cooking and eating it, in a symbolic sense, defines us, tells us and others about our attitudes and way of life.

Thus certain types of food define status (think of the difference between offering guests foie gras or TV dinners); others indicate tribal or national affiliations (the French call Englishmen *les rosbifs*; Englishmen disdain those frog eaters across the Channel; and most of the world thinks Americans live on burgers and apple pie); and other foods reflect regional vocabularies and attitudes (in Connecticut or California you *barbecue* a steak, while in the South *barbecue* is reserved for slow-cooked pork).

Grilling

Grilling meat and vegetables directly over flames or hot coals is the most ancient method of cooking. In its simplest form, meat is held over fire on a stick or propped up near the flames to cook in radiant heat. A more complex method is to build a grid of green sticks over the coals and lay food on it or to use a flat stone as a griddle over the fire. Modern grillers have simply replaced the sticks with skewers, the branches and flat stones with metal grills and grids. Virtually every kind of grilling or barbecuing or outdoor cooking we do today has its roots in the campfire cookery that hunter-gatherers practiced on those first hearths half a million years ago.

Roasting

Roasting in a campfire was achieved by burying the food to be cooked in hot ashes, often wrapped in leaves or mud, or by digging a pit, burying the food, and building a fire on top. Hawaiian luau cooks still prepare whole pigs by this method, and this is essentially what Southern pit barbecuers are doing when they slow-roast spareribs, pork shoulders, and beef briskets in their smoke-filled ovens. Cooking in a covered

kettle grill today reproduces this early pit roasting in which hot stones and coals raised the temperature in an enclosed space and cooked food in the superheated air.

Today grilling and barbecuing re-create these ancient ways of cooking. Ancestral memories surface when we build the fire and toss slabs of raw meat onto the grill. When the grill cook stands in a cloud of aromatic smoke and summons family and friends to the fire to share out portions of meat, we are not far from the hunter parceling out the kill around the campfire. The backyard barbecue enacts an ancient ritual, links us symbolically with our past.

Peter Farb and George Armelagos tell us in *Consuming Passions: The Anthropology of Eating*, "Only under special conditions—as when Western people consciously imitate an earlier stage in culture at a picnic, fish fry, cookout, or campfire—do they still tear food apart with their fingers and their teeth, in a nostalgic reenactment of eating behaviors long vanished. Today's neighborhood barbecue re-creates a world of sharing and hospitality. Nibbling on a roasted ear of maize gives us, in addition to nutrients, the satisfaction of participating in culturally simpler ways."

Grilling and Barbecuing: American Folk Arts

Anthropologists and folklorists talk about "-ways" that societies develop to create and organize their material cultures. Scholars look at what they call birthways or deathways or marriageways to study how different societies perform the rituals that define and create cultures. In recent years, students of American life have become increasingly interested in our foodways, the vocabulary, ingredients, and practices that make our cooking distinct from other cuisines and traditions.

In the 1930s the Works Progress Administration (WPA) created a project called the Federal Foodways Research Program to study the habits and traditions of food preparation and ingredients in America's varied regions. The intention, alas never realized, as World War II intervened and ended the study, was to provide a survey of American foodways to be published in a work to be entitled *America Eats*. The study did discover that there were major differences in styles of cookery that reflected regional attitudes and traditions and spawned a number of books and reports, which are described in *America Eats: Forms of Edible Folk Art*, by William Woys

Weaver. This fascinating book, named after the WPA project, focuses largely on the material artifacts of food culture such as pots and churns, but does provide some recipes for traditional dishes like corn dodgers and green tomato pie.

Weaver tells us how folklorists described a number of different regional cultures along the eastern seaboard, called "culture hearths," where "the various 'yeasts' of Old World folk culture rapidly hybridized to form something new and uniquely American." While these studies focused largely on architecture and furniture, Weaver feels that the same concepts can be applied to the culture of food: "Folk cookery, like folk architecture, is not the product of ethnicity, but rather part of a group's acquired cultural trappings, just as hoppin john has become a symbol of something intangible, something South Carolinian."

Each region developed its own particular style of cooking, its own vocabulary, customs, and traditions that defined the culture. And these traditions spread out as the country expanded from its colonial origins. Weaver says, "As Americans moved out of these regional settlement areas, they took their distinctive regional cultures with them and spread their folkways over a greater area of the United States. The basic patterns that molded American foods and eating habits as we know them today— Thanksgiving dinner, barbecued meats, milk on breakfast cereals, the hot dog, coffee drinking—evolved in these coastal settlement areas."

Barbecuing is first mentioned in the context of one of our emerging country's most important culture hearths, Virginia. Robert Beverly, writing in 1705 in his *History and Present State of Virginia*, describes this American way of cooking meat by "laying the Meat itself upon the Coals, or by laying it upon Sticks raised upon Forks at some distance above the live Coals, which heats more gently, and drys up the Gravy; this they, and we also from them, call Barbecuing."

The "they" and "them" that Beverly refers to in this passage are, of course, Native Americans. As Europeans settled in the new land they called America, they adopted ingredients and techniques from local Indians. Corn or maize is the food that is most identified with Indian agriculture, but early settlers drew on Native American culture for much of their sustenance, adopting foods such as squash, beans, potatoes, tomatoes, chiles, and turkeys that are so much a part of our cooking today.

When early settlers cooked meat outdoors they followed the Indian method of grilling food over hot coals on grids made of green branches. One settler, Thomas Griffith, travelling into the Cherokee Nation in the 1760s, tells us, "I bot some corn for my horse and potato bread and a fowl which I briled under a pine tree. I saw a hunter hawling in a Wild Turkey Cock that weighed 26 lb. when drawd." Griffith says he "briled" a fowl under a pine tree; Beverly uses a new word *barbecuing* to describe the same method of grilling food directly over the fire.

The word *barbecue* enters our language at the beginning of the eighteenth century and seems to be derived from a Taino or Arawak Indian word rendered by the Spanish colonists in the Caribbean as *barbacoa*. Thus *barbecue* refers to the grid of sticks that Beverly describes and that can be seen in the early engravings of Theodore de Brys that portray Indians grilling small animals over smoky fires. An early use of the word (1794) refers to a rack for sleeping, but barbecue usually referred to the grid upon which food is cooked and came to describe the practice of outdoor cooking in general in early America.

As time passed, barbecue came to mean not only the technique of grilling food over an open fire, but any outdoor gathering where grilled meats were eaten. Mary Moragné, a young belle from Carolina, describes a Fourth of July barbecue in 1839: "The family went in two carriage loads. This 'cue like all other 'cues consisted in eating a great deal and having a great deal more than could be eaten—although there were a great many persons present."

Barbecue soon came to be the name for political celebrations and election rallies where hungry (and thirsty) voters dined on sheep or hogs or whole oxen cooked over pits filled with burning coals and washed down with copious amounts of the local hooch. After one election-year barbecue, George Washington's campaign manager had to settle an immense bar bill for entertaining the voters with rum, beer, wine, and hard cider. At William Henry Harrison's campaign barbecue in the 1840s, voters ate 360 hams, 26 sheep, 20 calves, and 1,500 pounds of beef along with bread, cheese, pies, and lots of liquid refreshment. A sated Kentuckian described the feast at another nineteenth-century barbecue: "Here were five or six ditches dug two and a half feet deep, and about as wide, in which had been built fires, which when burned down to the coals, they had put over them quarters of veal and mutton upon spits of wood. . . . Further on was a table about two hundred feet long . . . strewed from end to end with . . . meat."

Barbecues Galore: American Political Feasts

"In the Colonial period, each region of the country had its own feasts connected with public events. In the Middle States, the sittings of the courts; May Day, when country boys decorated their heads with animal fur and went about the town shooting off guns; and fair days for the semi-annual markets were focal points for great social gatherings and considerable drinking. . . . Great bonfires were built and it was not unusual for one of the leading gentlemen in the community to organize an ox roast or bear roast, or 'barbecue,' as open-air roasting was then called. The high cost of such largesse was underwritten by the host as part of the obligation of his social position. In the shifting struggle for power and stature, it was a good way to acquire 'friends.' After the Revolution . . . the outdoor roasting customs were transferred to political rallies. At the presidential campaign rally for Harrison and Tyler held at Wilmington, Ohio, in 1840, 1,000 people gathered to raise a log cabin and consume corn dodgers, hard cider, and barbecued ham. . . . Election Day . . . gave the community a happy day of leisure filled with . . . drinking and socializing about the town common." (William Woys Weaver, *America Eats*)

The tradition of political barbecues continues to this day. Robb Walsh, in his *Legends of Texas Barbecue Cookbook*, describes Texas political barbecues from Sam Houston's "Great American Barbecue" in 1860 (to which all of Texas seems to have been invited) to LBJ's 1964 barbecue for the president of Mexico to a 1991 barbecue where twenty thousand guests feasted on eleven thousand pounds of beef. In Southern California, candidates for Los Angeles County sheriff have hosted enormous political barbecues over the years, serving thousands of prospective voters *barbacoa* (beef wrapped and roasted underground) and *carne asada* (grilled steaks), along with prodigious quantities of liquid refreshments.

But barbecuing didn't just take place on a grand scale at political rallies. It was also a feature of family dinners and communal get-togethers in early America. In 1775 Thomas Pickney, recruiting for the South Carolina militia, says that after speaking to settlers after Divine Service, he "finished the day on a barbecued beef." And Mary Randolph in *The Virginia House-wife*, written in 1824, gives us her recipe, "To Barbecue Shote" (see box below), which looks to be shoulder of pork roasted in a tangy sauce. Karen Hess, in her introduction to the book, says that here we see the origins of the sauces and mops that are characteristic of Southern-style barbecue: "The dryness of the meat noted by Beverly [in 1705] came to be compensated for by basting it with various mixtures. I cannot date this, but by the time of Mrs. Randolph's recipe 'To Barbecue Shote,' we find the meat baked in a sauce. In a sense, the sauce had already become the characterizing element of the barbecue, as it still is pretty much true today. Her rich sauce of 'Mushroom Catsup' and wine is eighteenth-century English. Today's fiery vinegary barbecue sauces may have originated in Creole [i.e., American, not European] customs."

"To Barbecue Shote"

"This is the name given in southern states to a fat young hog, which, when the head and feet are taken off, and it is cut into four quarters, will weigh six pounds per quarter. Take a fore quarter, make several incisions between the ribs, and stuff it with rich forcemeat; put it in a pan with a pint of water, two cloves garlic, pepper, salt, two gills of red wine, and two of mushroom catsup, bake it and thicken the gravy with butter and brown flour . . . if it be not sufficiently brown, add a little sugar to the gravy." (Mary Randolph, *The Virginia House-wife*)

While most research seems to focus on the Southern barbecue tradition, which emphasizes pork, we should realize that America has always been a steak-loving country. And the best way to cook a thick, tender steak, then and now, is by grilling it over a hot fire.

Mark Twain, pining in Europe for a real American steak, wrote:

Then there is the beefsteak. They have it in Europe, but they don't know how to cook it. Neither will they cut it right. It comes on the table in a small, round, pewter platter. It lies in the center of this platter, in a bordering bed of grease-soaked potatoes; it is the size, shape, and thickness of a man's hand with the thumb and fingers cut off. It is a little overdone, is rather dry, it tastes pretty insipidly, it rouses no enthusiasm.

Imagine a poor exile contemplating that inert thing . . . and imagine an angel suddenly sweeping down out of a better land and setting before him a mighty porter-house steak an inch and a half thick, hot and sputtering from the griddle; dusted with fragrant pepper; enriched with little melting bits of butter of the most unimpeachable freshness and genuineness; the precious juices of the meat trickling out and joining the gravy, archipelagoed with mushrooms; a township or two of tender, yellowish fat gracing an outlying district of this ample county of beefsteak; the long white bone which divides the sirloin from the tenderloin still in its place . . . could words describe the gratitude of this exile?

Grilled meat, especially steak, has long been a feature of the good life in America. In New York City immigrants feasted on prodigious amounts of grilled steak at "beefsteaks" or parties that encouraged diners to gorge on all the meat they could pack away. This largesse of meat would seem almost unbelievable to recent immigrants who in the old country ate meat only on special occasions. Hasia Diner, in her recent book *Hungering for America: Italian, Irish, and Jewish Foodways in the Age of Migration*, quotes an Italian immigrant remembering her childhood diet: "We ate *pan gialo* (corn bread), *minestra* (vegetable soup), pasta, polenta and meat maybe twice a year."

Colonists found a surplus of meat in the forests and fields of colonial America and often enjoyed it hot from the grill. European visitors wondered at the

amounts of meat consumed at American tables. Diner quotes an early English visitor: "As a flesh-consuming people, the Americans have no equal in the world. They usually have meat three times a day, and not a small quantity at each meal either. I have seen a gentleman choose as many as seven or eight different kinds of animal food from the bill of fare, and after having all arranged before him in a row, in the national little white dishes, commence at one end and eat his way through in half a dozen minutes."

America: Land of Plenty

America has always been seen as a rich and fertile land from the time when the first hunter-gatherers followed herds across the land bridge from Siberia to the nineteenth century, when European peasants arrived hungering for food and free land, to today, when people from third-world countries come looking for a new life.

And America offered settlers a plenitude of food. Early writers talked of being able to walk dry-shod over schools of fish, of forests teeming with game and fowl. Pioneers on the frontier in America could walk out into the woods and shoot a deer or a wild turkey; early settlers raised pigs that foraged for themselves and reproduced mightily. Eighteenth-century writers (James Fenimore Cooper has a famous passage in *The Prarie*) described flocks of passenger pigeons (now extinct from overhunting) that went on for miles. Farb and Amerlagos say in *Consuming Passions*, "Wild game provided meat for the eastern cities well into the nineteenth century. This primeval abundance affected the emerging cuisine of North America. It established the tradition of plenty that continued to this day."

Not only were the forests rich with game and the land fertile and abundant, no class of aristocrats controlled access to food and land they way they did in Europe. Land and food were readily available to new immigrants. We read in *The American Heritage Cookbook*: "Rich virgin lands were so cheap as to be had almost for the asking, but it cost plenty of back-breaking labor to clear them and bring them into cultivation. Still, the almost herculean effort was worth it and had high rewards. A man could be independent, his own master, beholden to no one and to nothing but the good green earth and his own industry and skills to provide his family with an ever-more-comfortable manner of life."

Food and Freedom

A Carolina settler wrote in a letter to relatives in England in 1701, "No strict laws bind our privileges. A Quest after Game, being as freely and peremptorily enjoyed by the meanest Planter Settler as he that is the highest in Dignity, or wealthiest in the Province. . . . A poor Labourer, that is Master of his Gun, hath a good a Claim to have continued courses of Delicacies crowded upon his Table, as he that is Master of a greater Purse."

Meat, above all, celebrated at beefsteaks in the North and barbecues in the South, could be eaten freely, in amounts that Europeans found staggering. Farb and Armelagos say that "the carnivorous tradition was . . . entrenched in North America. It was bolstered by the conditions of life on the frontier, which made killing wild game for food a necessity. The frontiersman entered the North American mythology as a symbol of masculinity, the crack shot who could always put meat on the table."

It's little wonder that our distinctly American style of cooking emphasizes meat or poultry or fish grilled over the fire or roasted in a smoky outdoor oven. We are celebrating the heritage that brought us here: protein-rich food, and plenty of it, cooked the way our forefathers cooked it, on a smoky fire, sharing the bounty of the land with family, friends, and neighbors.

And it's not at all strange that the North chose steak as its meat of choice and the South chose pork. The great flood of immigrants in the late nineteenth century coincided with the creation of the modern beef industry, in which the surplus beef of the West, fattened on corn in Midwestern feedlots, was shipped to the cities in the new refrigerated freight cars. Beef, and especially steak, was abundant in Eastern and Midwestern cities and new (and meat-hungry) Americans feasted on it. If you couldn't afford to grill a steak or roast a prime rib on Sunday, well, there was always pot roast or hamburger steak from cheaper cuts.

In the South pork was (and is) the preferred meat. Pigs were especially prolific; in the rich countryside and forests of the American South they multiplied so

quickly in colonial times that, as Beverly describes them in Virginia in 1705, "Hogs swarm like Vermine upon the Earth . . . [and] run where they list, and find their own Support in the Woods, without any Care of the Owner." Travellers complained that they were fed pork in various forms at every meal. The English writer Harriet Martineau, who journeyed through the South in the 1830s, griped about eating "little else than pork, under all manner of disguises."

The pig rules barbecue in the South. When you drive into Southern towns, images of fat and happy pigs grin from signs that say, "Barbecue Here." While you can usually find chicken at a barbecue pit, and almost all offer spicy sausage of some kind, usually called links, the pig is king. Regions vary, but preferred cuts of pork for the type of long and slow pit-roasted meat that Southerners insist is the only true barbecue are the shoulder and the spareribs. Both of these cuts are rather fatty and contain plenty of collagen or connective tissue that slow-roasting at low temperatures turns into gelatin, which gives Southern barbecue its characteristic luscious quality. You can certainly grill other cuts from the pig like loin chops or pork tenderloins, but you won't find it called barbecue, at least not in the South (see Barbecue: Who Owns the Word?, page 26).

The North's emphasis on beefsteak, grilled over the fire, and the South's predeliction for slow-cooked pork reflect the foodways of the two "culture hearths" that created our grilling and barbecuing traditions. But as the country spread west, we encountered another vibrant way of cooking food outdoors, the Southwestern and Mexican tradition of grill-cooking and pit-roasting typified by the *asaderos* or grill cooks.

We can see the traditions merging in Texas barbecue, where German butchers and black and Hispanic grill cooks drew on both Southern and Western foodways to roast highly seasoned beef in pit ovens and over smoky fires. While you can find pork shoulder and ribs slow-roasted Southern style, especially in east Texas, most Texas barbecue is based on beef. In modern times, the preferred cut is the tough, fatty brisket that turns silky and tender and smoky after hours in the barbecue pit.

Texas barbecuers and Hispanic *asaderos* often cooked whole steers or quarters of beef by burying the wrapped meat and building a fire on top. This ancient way of cooking is still found throughout the Southwest at ranch parties and fiestas. I remember a cookout and party when the parents of the students of my largely Hispanic high school in Los Angeles roasted quarters of beef by rubbing them with fiery chile powder and herbs, wrapping them in wet burlap, and burying them under a huge wood fire that burned slowly through the night. We kids sacked out in sleeping bags while our dads drank beer and talked, tending the fire all night long, telling stories, playing the guitar, singing *corridos*. The next day the beef was dug up, unwrapped and chopped, and served with salsa and beans cooked in huge Dutch ovens buried in the coals. The tender and spicy beef was a food epiphany for me. I never knew meat could taste that good.

Another traditional way of cooking beef in the Southwest was to dig a trench and burn mesquite or oak logs down into coals, then skewer large chunks of beef and slowly roast them in the smoke. The town of Santa Maria on California's central coast has made this type of grilling a specialty, with whole sirloins or, more recently, sirloin tri-tips, grilled and served to thousands of hungry diners at cookouts and festivals. Both methods of cooking, pit-roasting and grilling over coals, can still be done in offset smoker-cookers, water smokers, and kettle grills, although boards of health seem to have outlawed cooking meat by burying it, at least in professional operations.

One of the great advantages of the Hispanic tradition is the seasoning that is added to meat, chicken, fish, or vegetables, on or off the grill. Chiles in their various forms—fresh, dried, smoked, pickled, canned, or powdered—give grilled meat, poultry, or seafood a burst of flavor that is unrivaled. The versatility and range of flavors of chiles make them one of the great contributions of Native Americans to the world's cuisines— they are an essential part of the Southwestern grilling tradition. (See Chiles, page 60.)

When we get to California, we see Hispanic flavors and techniques every-where. Grilling was very much a part of Spanish life in the New World, and the tradition of the *asadero* is still strong on the *West Coast*. Helen Gurley Brown in *West Coast Cookbook* describes the fandangos and fiestas of early California: "Grilled meat was a part of every festive gathering. A large fire was made, a freshly killed beef hung in the shade of a tree, and *vaqueros* and their ladies cut off pieces every time that hunger called, and cooked it over the waiting fire. It wasn't only charcoal grilling that was practiced by those Californians of the past, they also had their huge pit barbecues even as today."

Grilling on the West Coast is also strongly influenced by Asian cooking styles and ingredients. Chinese cooks were the mainstay of western mining towns and

railroad camps, and many Pacific Coast restaurants to this day are staffed by Chinese cooks. Although Chinese chefs prefer stir-frying to grilling (Mongolian beef is the only grilled dish I can think of on Chinese restaurant menus), their ingredients and sauces are very much a part of the repertoire of West Coast cooking. Korean and Japanese cooks have strong traditions of food grilled over charcoal. In many Korean restaurants today, you can grill at the table your own thinly sliced beef, marinated chicken, or thin cuts of tender pork; the more adventurous can grill pieces of beef tongue or marinated beef intestine. Japanese grill restaurants are found in all West Coast cities, and here you find delicious fresh fish and seafood paired with traditional grill foods such as *yakitori*. Hawaiians love to grill fish, seafood, and chicken over *kiawe* wood (mesquite) and blend Asian and traditional Hawaiian ingredients in their cooking. Northwest Indians roast salmon on planks beside alder and cedar coals.

So in the West, barbecue takes on yet another meaning. It's still food cooked on a grid over coals, just like the original usage of barbacoa, in both the Spanish and the Asian traditions. And it can also refer to pit-cooking and roasting meat, as we see from the gargantuan feasts of wrapped, earth-cooked beef at fiestas and Western barbecues. But now we see signs in strip malls in Los Angeles that proclaim "Korean Barbecue." Grilling *bul goki* or marinated thin-cut short ribs at your table seems a long way from pulled pork in Carolina, but it's the same word with the same roots. Food and fire come together on the barbecue, wherever and however it's done.

The Backyard Barbecue in America: Dad as Grill Cook

While grilling food outdoors has always been a part of American life, the backyard barbecue as we know it is a recent invention. Soldiers returning home from World War II demanded access to the American Dream of a house and land. And government mortgage programs and builders of suburban communities like Levittown gave returning veterans and newly affluent factory workers the chance to own their homes. Although the land that was attached to these single-family homes could not really be measured in acres, the backyard, with its patio or deck and free-standing grill, gave many Americans access to an outdoor life that most city dwellers had only dreamed of. Soldiers who had endured K-rations and army food yearned for the steak and chicken and burgers that had filled their thoughts and dreams for years.

The development of lighter fluid in a can and charcoal briquettes made from compressed sawdust made cooking outdoors easy, and took away much of the mess and hassle that free-form charcoal or wood-fired grills entailed. Bottled barbecue sauce made it all even easier, although the sugar in these sweet sauces is largely responsible for that charred chicken too many of us remember from neighborhood barbecues.

All Dad had to do on Sunday afternoon was put charcoal briquettes in the backyard grill, spray on the lighter fluid, throw in a match, and stand back. When the fire was ready, he tossed on a few steaks and some corn on the cob, burgers or hot dogs or chicken pieces, brushed on the sauce, picked up his tongs, and he was a grill chef. Mom enjoyed it because all she had to do was make the potato salad and iced tea (and clean up afterward—Dad wasn't all that enlightened way back then). Kids loved it because eating outdoors was fun and an adventure and it was really a kick to see Dad, in a silly apron, actually cooking something.

And besides, the food, even with the char from the burnt sugar in the sauce and the elusive flavor of kerosene from the lighter fluid, was not out of the freezer or on a TV tray. It was real meat, that steak or burger or charred chicken, and you got to eat it outdoors with your hands and make a mess. There was (and is) an authenticity about grilled food that attracts us and links us to our roots. There's a little bit of the frontiersman in all Americans; a hint of our wild past still lingers amid all that smoke and meat.

With the advent of the kettle grill, invented by the Weber company in the 1950s from cut-up marine buoys, grilling became more sophisticated. Now the backyard cook was not simply a griller; he could also roast large pieces of meat or whole birds, and with a little care he could even slow-cook ribs to make Southern barbecue the way the professional pit man did. Wood chips and chunks opened up new possibilities with the kettle grill now becoming a smoker as well as a roaster. The kettle top also enabled the grill cook to control the fire more accurately and enabled him to use dampers and vents to quell the flare-ups that had burned so much chicken and steak on earlier backyard grills. The propane grill makes it all even easier by allowing precise temperature control,

although with a slight loss of the sense of wildness that accompanies a wood or charcoal fire, compensated, perhaps, by smoke from hardwood chips or chunks.

Since that time we have seen grill cookery take on even more complexity and sophistication. Now many restaurants have wood-burning grills to cook their meat, poultry, seafood, and vegetables. The backyard griller is no longer limited to steaks and burgers and chicken; the cook can now prepare a wide range of meats and birds, fish and seafood, and even vegetables and fruit on the grill. The modern outdoor cook can grill or roast or bake or smoke virtually any kind of food. Food on the fire is whatever you want it to be.

Barbecue: Who Owns the Word?

There are few words used in cooking today that generate as much controversy as *barbecue*. To many Americans barbecue is a general term for cooking anything on a grill outdoors. Thus you barbecue a steak on the grill, you sit down to a barbecued hamburger or barbecued corn at a picnic, you purchase a charcoal or a gas barbecue, you brush barbecue sauce on barbecuing chicken. (Aussies refer to shrimp on the barbie, but we won't go there.)

But there are some, upholders of the Southern tradition of pit-roasted barbecue (I call them the 'cue mafia when I'm in an argumentative mode), who feel that theirs is the only valid use of the word. These folks are very vocal in their defense of their heritage and will tell you that there is no such thing as a barbecued hamburger, that only pork shoulder or ribs or beef brisket (depending on where they are from and what regional tradition they are defending) is the true barbecue and all else is bogus.

One of the things I teach is language. Students are constantly asking why words keep changing meanings, why Shakespeare's English is so different from ours. *Cute*, for example, in earlier centuries and still today in urban slang denotes a sharp, cunning con man, while today most folks would use it to describe little kids all dressed up for the Easter parade. I point out to students that the Latin word *acutus*, or "sharp," lies behind the word and that it is a shortening of *acute*. Over the years the main meaning of the word shifted through usage from warning about a trickster to today's description of cute little kids, but the word retains some of its original meaning in slang. Barbecue, as a verb, adjective, and noun, like many words, has many meanings. People in one region can't say that their meaning is the only correct one, that they own the word barbecue, that they are right and everybody else is wrong. We just use the word differently.

Words mean what they mean because of usage. The dictionary does not create or freeze meaning; it only records how people have used a given word in different times and in different places. There is never any single, absolute, unchangeable meaning for any word anywhere. Language is constantly changing and evolving, and no one can be said to own any word—not for any length of time, that is. Teenagers keep trying to create and own words that their parents can't understand, but the words escape into everybody's language despite their efforts.

To understand how barbecue came to mean the backyard grill in much of America and spareribs and pulled pork in the South, we have to revisit our culinary history and see how the word originated in the South as a description of a rack used by Indians to cook food over a fire and evolved in the differing cultures and dialects of the North and South.

Regional Hearths

In colonial days, before Ben Franklin got around to inventing one, nobody had a stove. Cooking was done on the hearth, over hot coals burned down from firewood brought in from surrounding forests. Evan Jones, in his wonderful history of our country's cooking, *American Food: The Gastronomic Story*, tells us, "In Virginia, where life generally was easier—as well as in chilly New England—colonial housewives continued to prepare meals as their forebears had. Except for fair-weather days when they might cook outdoors, all their roasting, broiling, boiling, and baking were done in the blistering temperatures of the wide kitchen fireplace with its spits and its heat reflectors, its trivets, its drip pans, griddles, Dutch ovens, hanging pots and trammels and cranes, and its long-handled peels with which to recover food or containers buried in the coals."

If a colonial housewife wanted to broil a steak or roast a chicken, she used a grid or griddle to cook the piece of flat, tender meat directly on the fire, and, most likely, spit-roasted the chicken over a drip pan. Making stews, braising, and baking was

done in Dutch ovens placed among the coals with more coals heaped on top. Thus grilling and spit-roasting over the fire is basic to our American way of cooking, in the North and South. Cooks in the cooler North must have appreciated having a heat source like a hearth in the kitchen; Southern cooks probably found it unbearable during the hot summer months.

It's not surprising, then, that Southern cooks, mostly black slaves, many of whom were brought from the Caribbean to work on rice plantations in the Carolinas and in Virginia's tobacco fields, preferred to grill food outdoors over the barbacoa grids used by Indians and described by Virginia planter Robert Beverly in 1705. Cooking in the North, in homes, taverns, and restaurants, generally took place indoors, initially on the hearth and later on woodstoves. Southern kitchens were often not connected to the main house, and much of the cooking on large plantations was done outdoors or in the cookhouse.

A steak lover like Mark Twain, who lived in Connecticut in the latter part of the nineteenth century, longed for an American-style steak "hot and sputtering from the griddle," probably grilled on a stove indoors on a cast-iron griddle; Thomas Pickney dined on "barbecued beef" in South Carolina, almost certainly cooked outside. We see two regional traditions and two vocabularies emerging here: steak, chicken, and other meats were broiled on a griddle indoors and at clambakes, picnics, and political barbecues on outdoor grills in the North and Midwest; in the South, meat, especially pork, was barbecued over smoky wood fires in plantation cookhouses and at parties and political rallies. When Americans took to cooking outdoors in a big way after World War II, Northerners referred to whatever they cooked on the newfangled backyard barbecue grill, whether it was steak or chicken or burgers, as barbecued steak, chicken, or burgers; Southerners tended to limit their use of the word to traditional slow-cooked pork ribs or pork shoulder roasted in smoky barbecue pits.

Barbecue in the South: True 'Cue?

As professional pit men emerged in the South in the twentieth century, they provided this smoke-flavored, long-cooked pork to anyone who wanted to pay for it. Barbecue became a food identified with Southern life and traditions, and today it represents an

SPELLING BEE: IS IT BARBECUE OR BARBEQUE?

Since you've been reading this book, you already know I spell barbecue with a "c" and not a "q." The word entered into English from the Spanish rendition of the Caribbean Indian word, *barbacoa*, which is still the word for grilling and roasting outdoors in Mexico. The first uses of the word in English date back to the eighteenth century and were spelled with the "c." In 1824, a woman named Mary Randolph provided the recipe "To Barbecue a Shote" in *The Virginia House-wife*, and this seems to be the usage throughout the nineteenth century. In twentieth-century recipes we start to see the word spelled barbeque, most likely because spelling this looks French and therefore a bit more like *haute cuisine*. Another reason for using the "q" could be what the Oxford English Dictionary calls a "fanciful etymology"—deriving barbeque from the French phrase "*barbe à queue*," referring to the supposed *boucanier* (buccaneer or pirate) practice of roasting *bouc* (wild goats) from the *barbe* (beard) to the *queue* (tail) in the *boucan* (place used by Indians to smoke meat).

older, less hectic way of life than the fast-food joints that line the approaches to many American towns. Barbecue in the South has become a true folk art, with festivals and competitions attended by thousands of hungry folks who are vociferous in defense of their hometown cooks and traditional sauces. In October 2002, the Southern Foodways Alliance held a symposium called "Barbecue: Smoke, Sauce, and History" to discuss this traditional Southern way of cooking.

Most Southerners agree that pork is the king of 'cue, although there is some dispute as to whether spareribs should prevail over pork shoulder or the whole hog in some regions. But it's the sauce that really gets Southern barbecue fanciers arguing. As we saw in the recipe "To Barbecue Shote" from Mary Randolph's early cookbook, *The Virginia House-wife*, a spicy sauce has been a part of barbecue from the beginning. Evan Jones in *American Food* quotes a letter written in 1852 by Sarah Hicks Williams to her relatives back in New York after she journeyed to South Carolina to live on her husband's plantation: "Red pepper is much used to flavor meat with the famous 'barbecue' of the South and [the dish] which I believe they esteem above all dishes is roasted pig dressed with red pepper and vinegar."

Now, from this quote we could tell where Mrs. Willams's Southern relatives were from, even if Jones hadn't tipped us off in his footnote. We know the Williams plantation was located in Carolina because the roasted (most likely pit-roasted) pig was dressed with red pepper and vinegar, a typical Carolina-style mopping sauce. Each region has its own style of sauce: eastern North Carolina, near the coast, favors a sauce much like the one Mrs. Williams described, based on vinegar and red peppers; western North Carolina, in the Piedmont of the Appalachians, prefers a sauce that includes tomatoes along with the vinegar and peppers; in South Carolina these days they like to add yellow mustard to their vinegar-and-pepper–based sauce.

When we go farther north and west to Memphis or Kansas City, we begin to see sauces that are more like the standard barbecue sauce found on supermarket shelves. Memphis-style sauce, usually slathered on the smoky spareribs the city is famous for, is tomato-based, sweet and tangy and hot. Kansas City sauce is milder, sweeter, with a bit of hot pepper and spice mixed with tomatoes, vinegar, and molasses. As we move west into Texas, beef reigns supreme, with brisket the preferred cut of pit roasters. Some pit men in Texas use no sauce at all and prefer a rub made with chile powder, salt, and herbs. Others make a smoky, chile-and-tomato–based sauce that is influenced by the Hispanic tradition, like so much Texas and Southwestern food.

So the word *barbecue* in supermarket barbecue sauce refers a type of sweet basting and table sauce that resembles the sauces traditionally served in Memphis and Kansas City barbecue joints. This sauce became popular in the 1950s when it began to be commercially produced and it is now what most Americans call barbecue sauce. Folks in Carolina or Texas would disagree, of course. It is not their sauce, even though we all use the same word. But the word doesn't denote the same things. Who is right? Everybody's right: Barbecue sauce means different things in different regions, and that's just the nature of our language.

I might concede here that Southern 'cue fanciers could have a lock on the noun *barbecue* when it refers to food. When I say I'm going out to get some barbecue, I'm talking ribs, just like they are. And I certainly wouldn't describe a grilled burger as barbecue. I might call it a barbecued (adjective) burger, and I could also say I'm going to barbecue (verb) a burger on the barbecue (noun not referring to food). In my daily speech, I use *grilling* and *barbecuing* more or less as synonyms. Others differ, some vociferously, because their dialect is different from mine. Maybe we should all just relax a bit, put some good food on the fire to grill or barbecue, and enjoy ourselves.

Confessions of a Griller

It's hard to remember when I wasn't grilling food over some kind of fire. I spent my early years, during and right after World War II, in Westchester County, just north of New York City, where my father worked. It was an idyllic world, as I remember it, in a small community called Interlaken that surrounded a lake with plenty of swimming and fishing in summer and ice skating and wild hockey games in winter.

My life revolved around the lake and the surrounding woods. As soon as I could read, my father gave me a book by a writer of frontier novels. His main character, a combination of the Deerslayer and Daniel Boone I suppose, roamed the dark and bloody ground of Kaintuckee, hunting and fishing and fighting Indians. I soon decided that this was the life for me, and that I would wander the forest, with my compass and jackknife and fishing rod, living off the land and having adventures.

I would, of course, lie to my sainted mother, bless her, and tell her I was going down to the lake to do a little fishing. Then I would simply take off into the woods with my compass in whatever direction my fancy took me. I would catch perch and sunfish and crappie and the occasional bass whenever I could in small slate blue lakes or the little streams that fed them. These became my forest meals, cooked as my hero in the book did over a tiny Indian-style fire that I kindled with sticks and brush and matches stolen from the kitchen.

I'd gut the small fish with my knife, skewer them on sharpened willow branches, and hold them over the flames until nicely charred. The hot flesh, picked carefully from among the burned skin and many bones, and eaten with what I hoped were wild onions plucked from the stream bank, tasted better than the sandwiches my mother had lovingly packed for me. Like St. Augustine's stolen pears that were sweeter than those from his family's tree, this wild food eaten alone in the woods satisfied a yearning in me, even at that young age, to be out in nature, a lone hunter by a fire, dreaming of a past life.

When we moved to Los Angeles, my family bought a house right at the southwestern edge of the city. Beyond the city limits was a world of dry brush and oil wells, irrigation ditches and truck farms, now a vast expanse of homes and patios and shopping centers. We neighborhood kids roamed this lost frontier with BB guns and slingshots, hunting whatever moved: jackrabbits, quail, meadowlarks, lizards, rattlesnakes, each other. Just about all we ever killed with our limited weaponry were lizards, and none of us felt that these mangled blue-bellied beings were particularly edible. Fishing was another story, however. We caught bluegills and catfish in the catch ponds that fed the irrigation ditches for the small farms owned by Chicano families whose chickens we were always hungering for but never could figure out how to catch.

We'd cook our fish over campfires on grills we made from racks filched from abandoned iceboxes. We just piled up fallen branches from the trees that circled the ponds, lit them with the everhandy stolen kitchen matches, and tossed the gutted fish on the grill. Seasoning was salt, again purloined from our mothers' kitchens and hidden in jars in the rocks by the pond, and cans of chiles we bought at the tiny stores that sold candy and soda pop and beer to wandering bands of kids, farm workers, bikers, hoboes, and oilfield roustabouts.

As we grew up we expanded our circle of wandering to include the desert and mountains surrounding the Los Angeles Basin. We shot rabbits and quail in the desert and roasted them over sagebrush and manzanita fires. Trout from mountain lakes we'd grill over oak and pine fires burned down to coals. One of Hollywood's most famous Western actors was my scoutmaster in the Boy Scouts (this being Los Angeles), and we'd camp with his sons at Vasquez Rocks, a favorite Western movie location in the nearby desert, grilling hamburgers on the campfire, telling ghost stories, keeping warm on cold winter nights beside huge bonfires of burning truck tires.

During my years at St. Mary's College in the hills east of San Francisco Bay (where I teach today and man the grill at student and faculty barbecues), I kept on cooking. I worked in the kitchen to pay for my board and ended up as assistant cook to a burned-out chef whose bouts with the bottle kept him from doing much except telling me how to cook two hundred steaks for famished students while he slumped by the grill. A good part of my college years was spent standing in smoke while Chef rapped out the orders and I flipped the burgers, enjoying every minute of it and eating all the leftovers.

These cooking skills came in handy during the years after college when I roamed around Europe and America, studying languages, literature, and philosophy, often making a living by cooking in restaurants and college kitchens. I retuned to the Bay Area just as the food revolution was taking off and combined college teaching with being part-owner, assistant chef, waiter, maitre d', and occasionally bouncer in a rollicking restaurant and nightclub that combined Cajun food, political theater and cabaret, zydeco music, and rock and roll.

I bought an old house in Oakland on what was then an urban frontier with gunshots in the night and police helicopters rattling overhead. I started out raising rabbits, chickens, and vegetables in an attempt to become self-sufficient with my growing family on my third-of-an-acre plot. While the urban homesteading didn't work out as intended (no kids will ever eat a rabbit they've seen grow up, and raccoons ate up all the chickens in one night), I did (and do) a lot of outdoor cooking in the huge yard and garden that surround the house. Over the years I've dug pits and roasted whole lambs and suckling pigs over coals, cooked *cabrito* (kid) on a spit, and grilled innumerable steaks, burgers, chickens, turkeys, and fish on every kind of homemade or store-bought barbecue imaginable.

I still do most of my cooking outdoors. I use a large kettle-style charcoal grill and a propane gas grill for most grilling and have a water smoker for long and slow barbecuing. I grill mostly meat and fish and poultry since grilling is a style of cooking that is quick and easy and healthy, and above all, it tastes good. I seem to want the flavor of the fire in just about anything I cook. My tomato crop is prodigious this summer, and my habit these days is simply to grill five or six tomatoes for a few minutes along with slices of onion and chop them together with some basil and garlic from the garden. This becomes dinner for me and my wife, Kathy, along with a little pasta and some grilled fish or meat or chicken. And bread and wine, of course. Angelo Pellegrini, author of *Lean Years, Happy Years* and one of my heroes, tells us that all we need in life is family and a garden and a place to eat what it grows. I'd include a grill and a bottle of wine, but that about sums it up. Voltaire was right: The good life is found when you cultivate your own garden. And grill what it gives you.

Grilling Techniques and Equipment

Grilling is direct cooking of small pieces of fish, meat, poultry, vegetables, or fruit over high heat. If you try to grill a big chunk of meat or a whole bird directly over a hot fire, by the time it is cooked on the inside, it will most likely be charred and inedible on the outside. Thus the best foods for direct grilling are relatively tender, relatively thin pieces of meat, poultry, fish, vegetables, or fruit. Hamburgers and steaks, chops and fish fillets, thin pieces of poultry such as boneless chicken breast or thighs, sliced zucchini or eggplant, pieces of tender fruit such as peaches or pears are all suitable for grilling over direct heat.

Roasting, since it cooks all surfaces at a controlled rate, can allow for more time to let the interior cook through while the surface gradually browns. Thus larger pieces of meat or whole birds, whole fish or large fish fillets, and even pizza or other breads and pastries can be roasted or baked on today's kettle grills using indirect heat where the fire is spread out around a central, unheated portion of the grill. Some tougher cuts of pork and beef are best roasted at very low temperatures in smoky fires to produce the savory barbecue found throughout the South. This technique of long, slow cooking or slow-roasting calls for special attention to temperatures and woodsmoke; it often requires special smoker-cookers, but can be done on kettle grills with some care and effort.

A combination of grilling and roasting is the best way to cook some foods. Here larger pieces of poultry such as chicken quarters or halves, very thick steaks and chops, whole pork tenderloins, medium-sized fish or large shellfish such as lobster are first seared over direct heat, and then moved to a cooler or unheated portion of the grill to finish cooking. The kettle grill is ideal for this type of cooking, since it allows for both direct grilling, roasting by indirect heat, or a combination of the two. When you build a charcoal fire with three heat levels or light up a gas grill with multiple burners, you can control the amount of heat under different areas of the grill to allow for any type of grilling or roasting.

Grilling

Since grilling involves the application of high heat directly to the food, when you build your charcoal fire or light up the gas grill, you should create at least one portion of the fire with high (375°F to 400°F) to very high (400°F to 450°F) heat levels. A quick test of heat that many grill chefs use: Hold your hand a few inches over the grill and start counting slowly. If you have to remove your hand by the count of 3, you have a hot fire. If you can only get to 2, the fire is very hot. If you can get to 4 or 5, you have medium-hot to medium fire. For most direct grilling, it's best to have three levels of heat on the grill, one area of high heat, one with a lower temperature level, and another with no heat underneath. (See Building a Fire, page 39.) This will enable you to move food around as it cooks and to avoid flare-ups by moving food in danger of charring to a cooler or unheated portion of the grill.

Grill most small pieces of fish and shellfish directly over very high heat. Steaks and chops less than 1½ inches thick should be cooked over high heat; hamburgers, thicker steaks, chops, and thin pieces of chicken over medium high (350°F) to medium (325°F) heat. Direct grilling can be done successfully on hibachis, small grills without covers, and on stovetop grills, in addition to charcoal or gas-fired kettle grills. There is some discussion as to whether you should or should not cover kettle grills when grilling over direct heat. Some feel that covering the grill creates an unpleasant burnt-fat flavor in food. I've never found this to be the case, as I usually add wood chips or chunks to the fire to create plenty of woodsmoke, and I routinely cover my kettle grill when cooking on direct heat. I think covering the grill helps cook the food and also is a good control for flare-ups. Follow your own preference here.

Combination Grilling-Roasting

Combining grilling and roasting is a good technique for cooking larger pieces of chicken, duck or turkey along with pork chops or pork tenderloins that should also be cooked through to the center. When you build a charcoal or hardwood fire (see Building a Fire, page 39), be sure to create three levels under your grill: high heat, medium-high heat, and no heat. When you use a gas grill with multiple burners, turn one to the highest heat, one to medium-high and turn off one burner. Sear the food directly on high heat to seal the surface and create a tasty crust, then move the meat to the cooler or unheated portion of the grill to continue cooking until done.

You will need a kettle grill for combination grilling-roasting and you should cover the grill from the beginning to let the food get the full benefit of the roasting process. For most foods cooked this way, you will usually not need to place a drip pan under the unheated portion of the grill, although particulary fatty pieces of poultry or meat might require one to catch the grease.

Indirect Grilling or Roasting

You need a kettle or other type of covered grill for outdoor roasting. Build a charcoal or hardwood fire with two piles of charcoal on either side of a central portion of the grill (see Building a Fire, page 39). For a gas grill, light burners on either side of an unheated portion of the grill. Place a drip pan underneath the unheated area. Some grill manufacturers make foil drip pans in large (9 x 13") and small (6 x 8½") sizes. These not only work well as drip pans, but are also very handy for baking cobblers and crisps and for braising on the grill (see Braising, page 38).

Place the food on the unheated portion of the grill over the drip pan and roast in a covered grill until done. With a charcoal grill, you might need to add more briquettes or pieces of charcoal to maintain the desired temperature. You will often have to add more wood chips or chunks to keep the smoke going (see Woodsmoke and Herb Smoke for Flavor, page 43). Most foods roast best at medium-high (350°F) to medium (325°F) temperatures so that the heat will have time to penetrate to the center. Some foods (see below) require long, slow cooking to be tender and juicy. Smoke-roasting is a term often used by barbecue chefs and grillers. It is basically indirect grilling or roasting with plenty of smoking materials added at the beginning of the process and throughout the roasting period for maximum smoky flavor.

Long, Slow Cooking or Slow-Roasting

When a Southerner talks of barbecue, this is what he's talking about. Southern barbecue is usually pork shoulder or spareribs (although Texans barbecue beef

brisket, and virtually everybody serves up chicken and sausage links) slow-cooked in a smoky fire for many hours. Although you can cook at relatively low temperatures in a kettle grill, long, slow cooking is best achieved by using a pit cooker or offset smoker-cooker or water smoker (see pages 46–47) that can reproduce the low temperature roasting achieved by professional barbecue pit men all over the South. And by low, they mean keeping the temperature at 200°F to 250°F, a temperature range that is difficult to achieve on today's kettle grills (about the lowest temperature you can easily maintain in a kettle grill is 250°F to 300°F). And slow means 8 to 10 to 12 to as many as 20 hours for some large pieces of meat, not the amount of time most backyard grillers want to spend.

This type of cooking is not for everyone, obviously, and you wonder if it's worth the effort until you bite into a tasty pulled pork sandwich or tuck into a plate of luscious, smoky brisket. I've included a number of slow-roasting recipes in this book (Slow Cooked Spareribs, Two Ways, page 126, Carolina Pulled Pork, page 130, Pork Shoulder Roast with Five-Pepper Rub, page 129, and Texas Style Brisket, page 154). I provide two ways to cook these dishes: Method I by long, slow roasting in an offset smoker-cooker or water smoker and Method II by roasting at moderately low temperatures in a kettle grill for 2 to 3 hours. These slow-roasted dishes often use mops and sauces that are applied during cooking or toward the end to add extra flavor and moisture to the meat.

Braising

Braising is a technique that involves browning meat and then cooking it with some liquid in a covered pot. Braising in wine or beer with spices and herbs tenderizes tough cuts like beef short ribs and creates a wonderful gravy. I've experimented with a cowboy technique of campfire cooking where tough cuts of beef are braised in a Dutch oven buried in the coals. Browning short ribs over a smoky fire and them putting them into a Dutch oven or foil-wrapped drip pan and braising over indirect heat in a kettle grill reproduces this campfire cookery (see Cow Country Dutch Oven Short Ribs, page 156, and Campfire Beans, page 150). I've been having fun trying this technique on the grill and you might want to give it a try with your favorite stews and braises.

Building a Fire

The key to creating the fire in a grill or barbecue is to suit the fire to the style of cooking you intend to do. You should create the heat levels and fire configuration suited to what you are cooking: A small piece of fish will require a very hot concentrated fire, while spareribs will need a slow, dispersed source of heat and smoke. While there are some true believers who feel that only one type of heat source will do, to me heat is heat and the choice of the source is up to you. Charcoal (briquettes or free-form), hardwood logs, and propane or natural gas all have their adherents. You can acheive special effects with some fuels (mesquite charcoal, for example provides a very hot fire), but they by and large achieve similar results. By using hardwood chips or chunks, it's simple to add smoky flavors to virtually any type of outdoor heat source (See Woodsmoke and Herb Smoke for Flavor, page 43).

Charcoal Briquettes

Briquettes made from compressed sawdust are by far the most convenient form of charcoal. They are easy to light and burn evenly and efficiently. Briquettes are suitable for all kinds of grill cookery from direct grilling over high heat to long, slow roasting. Some briquettes now contain bits of hardwood that can add smoke and wood flavor to the food. Briquettes can be lit using commercial lighter fluid, but some feel these kerosene-based fuels add an unpleasant flavor to the food and are harmful to the environment. If you do use them, be sure that they have burned off fully before putting food on the grill.

My preferred method of lighting briquettes is with a chimney starter. These are easy to use: Simply fill the top compartment with briquettes and put crumpled newspaper in the bottom compartment. Light the newspaper and let it burn to ignite the charcoal. When the charcoal is thoroughly ignited, either use it to light more charcoal or spread the burning coals on the grid as needed. Weber now makes a large chimney starter that contains enough charcoal for most fires without having to add any more briquettes. Electric starters also work well. Follow the manufacturer's directions and be sure to remove the starter immediately after the coals ignite.

To create the three-level fire described above for direct grilling and combination grilling-roasting, pile lit coals two or three levels deep on one side of the fire

grid for high or very high heat, pile coals one or two levels deep for low to medium heat, and leave one portion of the grid without any coals for low to no heat. Thus you can move food from hotter to cooler or unheated areas of the grill to avoid flare-ups and to make sure food cooks to the desired level of doneness.

For indirect grilling or roasting: Divide lit coals into two piles pushed to either side of the fire grid underneath the grill handles so that more coals and/or hardwood chips or chunks can be added through the holes, Or spread the coals in a circle around the edge. In either case, leave an unheated center area on the fire grid where you can put a drip pan beneath the food to be roasted on the grill above. Adjust the amount of coals to create the desired heat level: 25 or more briquettes on either side should get you a moderately hot fire; 12 or less will result in medium to low temperatures. Follow the manufacturer's directions, use an oven or built-in thermometer, and experiment as you go. If you are roasting for more than an hour or so, add more briquettes as needed to the fire through the holes under the handles. Some kettle grills now come with a hinged grill that enables you to add more coals or hardwood chips or chunks easily.

Free-form Charcoal

Free-form charcoal is the original type of charcoal. Charcoal is made from hardwood logs that have been charred in an oxygen-free environment to remove water and other materials and leave a relatively pure form of flammable carbon. You can find many types of hardwood charcoal in the market: oak, hickory, and mesquite are the most common. Free-form charcoal burns hotter that briquettes since there is more oxygen available and it throws off a lot more sparks. It takes getting used to and can be dangerous in fire-prone areas, but hardwood charcoal provides a smoky undertone that many prefer. I use free-form mesquite charcoal, easily found in California, to broil fish and seafood since I like the high heat and tangy smoke flavor it provides. I don't usually use free-form charcoal for indirect grilling or roasting, especially when I want low temperatures, as it burns quickly and needs to be replenished often. Follow the directions for briquettes on page 39, for lighting and spreading free-form charcoal on the fire grid.

Hardwood

Some people swear by hardwood logs and feel that this is the only authentic way to get real smoke flavor in food. I'm not convinced, but hardwood does provide plenty of flavor after it's burned down to coals and it works especially well with foods cooked by indirect grilling or roasting. Those who cook with offset smoker-cookers (see below) often use hardwood logs in the fire-box and sometimes mix hardwood logs with charcoal for their long, slow, and smoky style of cooking.

To create a bed of hardwood coals: Ignite the logs by using kindling and newspapers and let them burn down to coals. Arrange the coals you would as charcoal, above, as needed for the type of grilling you intend to do. If you are cooking for a considerable amount of time, you might want to kindle another hardwood fire in another barbecue to feed live coals to the fire. Preferred woods for hardwood cooking are oak, hickory, pecan, and fruitwoods such as apple.

Gas

Propane or natural gas kettle grills are increasingly popular and provide excellent results for most grilled foods. The advantage of gas-fueled grills is ease of use and convenience; they make it easy to turn on the grill when you come home from work and want to grill some seafood or a chicken breast for a light and healthy dinner on the deck. I use my gas grill, conveniently located on a small deck just off my kitchen, for anything I want to grill quickly such as steaks, pork tenderloins, lamb chops, vegetables, and most seafood. My charcoal grill seems to give better results for smoke-roasting foods like pork loin or whole chickens, providing more smoke flavor and a crisp surface, although I often cook chickens or pork roasts with good results on the rotisserie on the gas grill. When I want to cook long and slow—pork shoulder or spareribs—I either use my charcoal kettle grill or my water smoker (see page 47).

One advantage of charcoal grills over gas grills is that it is easier to ignite hardwood chips and keep them burning at low to medium temperatures (see Woodsmoke and Herb Smoke for flavor, page 43). One trick: don't soak the chips before you put them in a gas grill and avoid hardwood chunks altogether. Gas grills don't often provide the really high heat you need for grilling fish like ahi tuna or

salmon steaks that you want to serve rare or medium-rare; I usually use hot-burning mesquite charcoal in the kettle grill for these fish, although they can be cooked with good results on preheated gas grills.

To prepare for cooking in a gas grill, follow the manufacturer's directions, which usually involve preheating the grill with all burners on and the cover closed. I have a three-burner grill (and I would not recommend any gas grill with less than three burners) arranged horizontally and I like to let the grill heat to about 375°F before cooking. While the barbecue heats up I clean the grill surface thoroughly with a cellulose or wire brush to remove any bits of food or accumulated grease. I also stoke the woodbox with hardwood chips or put a packet of wood chips on one of the burners (see Woodsmoke or Herb Smoke for Flavor, page 43).

Once the grill is preheated, prepare the fire for the type of cooking you intend to do. If I want to grill thin fish fillets or small pieces of seafood such as shrimp, I let the grill heat up to 400°F or more and leave all the burners on, since I want maximum heat and don't expect to get many flare-ups. If the fish is very oily, like escolar or salmon for example, or has been marinated in an oil-based marinade, you might want to turn one burner off to provide a place to move the food if flare-ups occur.

For most other direct grilling where I want to end up with rare or medium-rare food (steaks and lamb chops, for example, or thicker fish fillets and most vegetables), I leave two burners in the front on high and turn off the burner in the back (follow your own grill's configuration here; just leave two burners on and one off). Thus I can grill quickly on high to medium high heat, and move food to the unheated area if there are flare-ups. For foods that you want to cook longer and want to serve medium to well done (hamburgers, chicken pieces, pork tenderloin, and pork chops), set up the burners for combination grilling-roasting by turning one burner to high to medium-high, another medium to low, and turn one off. You then can sear the food over higher heat to create a savory crust, and move it to the area with lower or no heat to finish cooking without burning the surface.

Indirect grilling or roasting is simple on a gas grill. Simply turn off the middle burner, whether the burners are horizontally or vertically configured, leaving the center of the grill unheated. Put a drip pan underneath the unheated portion and follow the directions in the recipe. Most rotisserie attachments require you to remove the grill when you set up the spit and drip pan, but follow the manufacturer's directions here.

Woodsmoke and Herb Smoke for Flavor

One of the great attractions of grill cookery is the flavor of smoke from the fire. It's the smoke, I think, that provides us with a nostalgic hint of past campfires and adds a wild undertone to the food we grill. If you grill over hardwood logs or charcoal, you'll get a flavor from the wood itself, but most of us add smoke flavor using hardwood chips or chunks. Many types of wood chips and chunks are widely available now and can be purchased in markets and hardware stores, from specialty retailers, and by mail order (see Sources, page 200). Pellets of compressed hardwoods that are added to the fire in aluminum foil pouches are also coming onto the market.

If you are using charcoal, either briquettes or free-form, or hardwood coals in a kettle grill, the process is simple. Soak hardwood chips or chunks in water to cover for at least 30 minutes before adding them directly to the coals. Replenish chips or chunks as needed by putting them through the holes under the grill handles or by lifting the grill carefully and placing the soaked wood pieces directly on the hot coals. Chips or chunks will only work in a covered grill; they will flame up and burn without providing much smoke flavor in an open grill.

Most gas grills come with an optional smoker box, which I strongly recommended purchasing with your grill. Follow the manufacturer's directions or place unsoaked wood chips in the smoker box when you are preheating the grill. I have not been able to use hardwood chunks in a gas grill, but perhaps some grill manufacturer will come up with a way. Cover the gas barbecue for smoke flavor whether you are grilling directly or indirectly.

If you are cooking by indirect heat or roasting at medium heat levels or below in a gas grill, it is sometimes difficult to ignite and keep wood chips burning to create enough smoke for flavor. If you don't have a smoker box or are having trouble keeping chips going in a gas grill, make a packet about 4 inches square from heavy-duty aluminum foil, place a handful of chips on the foil, and fold to seal the packet. Poke a number of holes in the top and bottom of the packet and place it directly over one of

the burners underneath the cooking grill. In a little while, the chips should start smoldering and provide enough smoke to flavor the food. This is the same technique that most manufacturers of pelletized hardwood recommend with their products. Add more packets as needed as the food cooks. Be careful discarding packets; make sure the chips or pellets are fully extinguished before you throw them away.

Each variety of hardwood adds its own flavor to food. Experiment with various types to see which you prefer with different meats, poultry, fish, or seafood. Be sparing with the smoke at first as some woods have pronounced flavors that can overpower delicate foods. Never use pine or any softwoods as they can contribute an unpleasant resiny character. Only use wood that you know the origin of; do not use wood discarded from building sites as it could contain harmful additives.

Here are some of my favorite smoke and food combinations:

Oak has a powerfully flavored smoke and adds a sweet, woody undertone to pork and beef and is also excellent with turkey or chicken.

Hickory is a nutty-flavored smoke and is my favorite with pork of any kind; it's my preferred wood with long, slow roasted pork shoulder and smoke-roasted pork loin.

Pecan is the wood used by many Southern pit men, and gives pork, ham, and chicken a smoky, nutty flavor that is unforgettable.

Mesquite gives off a tangy, lightly spicy smoke that is wonderful with grilled steak and slow-cooked brisket. I like mesquite with grilled lamb and find it irresistible with grilled fish, especially chile-accented escolar or shark.

Alder is the favorite wood of Northwest Indian grill cooks, who smoke salmon in this slightly sweet smoke. Great for all seafood, it also adds a subtly smoky undertone to chicken or turkey.

Apple gives off a mild, fruity smoke that is perfect for delicate foods such as seafood and chicken. It is also excellent with pork tenderloin, especially when the meat is flavored with a sweet and savory marinade or glaze.

Herbs

Woody herbs such as thyme, rosemary, fennel, oregano, and marjoram create wonderfully aromatic smoke when added to the fire. Soak the stems and attached leaves in water to cover for at least 1 hour and then add them to the coals or on top of the burners in a gas grill. Cover the grill and let the smoke billow up around the food. Thyme, oregano, and marjoram go especially well with beef and pork, rosemary with lamb, and fennel is a classic accompaniment to grilled fish.

Equipment

The equipment you grill with can be as simple or elaborate as you want, from a small hibachi on a balcony to a built-in behemoth in the backyard with all the bells and whistles. You can cook all the direct-grilling recipes in this book using an open grill such as a hibachi or a stovetop grill, but for best results with most recipes I strongly recommended a kettle grill with a cover. Some companies make small charcoal or gas kettle grills these days that are suitable for outdoor cooking in restricted spaces. These work well, although I'm told that the manufacturer of at least one of the small, covered gas grills does not recommend using wood chips for adding smoke flavor.

Kettle Grill   This is standard equipment for most backyard grillers these days. Charcoal-fueled covered grills come in a wide variety of sizes and shapes, although the bench-mark remains the round Weber barbecue that started the whole phenomenon of grill roasting in the 1950s. The advantages of the cover are many: control of the fire by using dampers and vents, ease in dealing with flare-ups, and most important, the ability to roast in the grill using indirect heat. One disadvantage of the most popular brand of kettle grills is that the fire-grid is not adjustable. I don't find that a problem, since I employ the three-level fire recommended earlier (see Building a Fire, page 39) and control heat levels by opening or closing vents on the top and bottom of the grill. Some of the more expensive types of kettle grills come with an adjustable fire grid and many grillers swear by them.

Gas Grill   Increasingly popular today are covered grills fueled either by propane tanks or by natural gas. Some purists insist that you should always grill or barbecue over a "live" fire of charcoal or wood, but I've been using a propane grill for the last few years, in addition to my charcoal grill, and it works well for me and my family. The

gas grill is extremely easy to use and only requires turning on the burners and cleaning off the grill surface to get grilling. I almost always add hardwood chips of some kind to the smoker box, an essential part of my grill; the smoker box is an add-on that I think is worth buying with any gas grill, although you can add chips to the gas grill in pouches of heavy-duty foil (see Woodsmoke and Herb Smoke for Flavor, page 43).

Thus I get the convenience of the gas grill with the smoke flavor associated with the live fire. I admit I lose a bit of the wildness of the charcoal or wood fire, but I find that I can create plenty of smoky flavor in just about all the foods I grill. Added evidence: Almost all of my T-shirts in summer and sweatshirts in winter retain the smell of smoke. I'm getting so I can even identify the type of hardwood chips I used by the smell of the shirt: There's the mesquite from last night's porterhouse; this one is definitely hickory from the baby back ribs the night before.

Offset Smoker-Cooker Barbecue fanatics will tell you that you can't make true Southern-style barbecue without one of these contraptions, although I've cooked plenty of delicious 'cue on my covered grill. The principle of the offset smoker-cooker, often called a pit cooker, is that you create your heat and smoke in one compartment and convey the smoke and a regulated amount of heat to another compartment where the food is cooked. This way you can get plenty of smoke flavor into the food while it cooks at very low temperatures (usually around 200°F or lower). It is difficult to maintain such low temperatures for any length of time in a cooker where the heat source is in the same space as the food. Thus the standard covered charcoal or propane grill just can't keep the heat low enough for the long, slow cooking and smoking that Southern pit men insist is necessary for the luscious spareribs or pork shoulder or beef brisket they serve.

Most kettle grills can keep the temperatures at or about 250°F to 300°F, and I've provided a method for cooking classic barbecue in this temperature range. In the Southern and Texan barbecue recipes in this book, you'll find Method I, which describes how to cook at very low temperatures in an offset smoker-cooker or a water smoker (see below) and Method II, which gives you instructions for cooking delicious barbecue in a kettle grill at temperatures in the 300°F range. Mail order vendors of offset smoker-cookers, and other grills, are found in Sources (page 200).

Water Smoker The water smoker is a variation on the charcoal kettle grill that interposes a pan filled with water between the fire grid and the grill on which the food is placed. Thus the heat of the cooking compartment is tempered by the water and temperatures can be kept low for long cooking in a moist, smoky environment. Water smokers work well for slow-cooked barbecue and for smoking foods like chicken, turkey, or salmon. I use mine whenvever I am looking for an intense, smoky flavor in food that I want to cook for a long time.

To use a water smoker follow the manufacturer's directions or start a large (up to 5 pounds for my water smoker) charcoal fire on the fire grid and fill the pan with water or other liquid. Add soaked hardwood chunks or small hardwood logs (most chips will burn up too quickly) to the fire, place the food on the top grid, cover, and cook until done. Water smokers will usually give you relatively high heat levels at the beginning, which will brown the meat, and then progressively lower levels as the fire burns down. Experiment with your own equipment and use a built-in or oven thermometer to read the temperature in the cooking compartment and an instant-read meat thermometer to monitor doneness in the food.

Kamado The kamado is a Japanese earthenware grill or charcoal oven that looks like a large, handsome pot with a domed lid. Kamados require some experimenting and artistry to cook food on successfully, but I have friends who swear by them. I have had some amazingly good roasted chicken, lamb, and turkey cooked on kamado grills and I've often thought of getting one. Like chess, however, or more correctly, the game of *go*, I keep putting off learning until I have the leisure time to try to become a master.

Hibachis and Other Uncovered Grills There are any number of inexpensive, small uncovered grills on the market today. The hibachi is the most common and it can be a good grill for a small balcony or any place outdoors where space is tight. Small covered grills are available from many manufacturers, so I don't really

see why someone would want to buy a hibachi or any grill without a cover. But if you just want to grill a bit of fish or skewered meat or vegetables, a hibachi-style grill will do fine. Large uncovered backyard barbecues or braziers are still sold, but I see no sense in buying one of these when you can get a kettle grill for about the same price.

Stovetop Grills Cast iron or other metal grills or ridged pans are a good way to grill small pieces of meat, fish, or poultry on a stove indoors. These fit over one or two burners on the stovetop and can be used to grill steak or chops or a fish fillet or two easily and quickly. They do require ventilation, however, as grilling causes smoke, especially if the food is at all fatty or has been marinated in oil. If you have a ventilation fan and can't grill outside, a stovetop grill is a good alternative to a charcoal or gas grill.

Campfire Cooking Cooking over the coals of an open fire is our most ancient cooking technique, and fishermen, hunters, and hikers are still preparing delicious food over campfires. I'm sure most campers have their own techniques: mine was (and is) to build a hardwood fire and let it burn down to coals, prop a rack on four stones arranged around the coals, and grill the trout (if I've been lucky) or the hot dog or burger (if I've been skunked). Dutch ovens and aluminum foil packets can be used for roasting, baking, and braising on the campfire.

Rotisserie I think that the rotisserie attachment sold with many gas or charcoal kettle grills is a good addition to the grill cook's repetoire. I use the rotisserie with my gas grill often, to spit-roast chickens, pork loin, boned and rolled lamb leg, and beef fillet. The trick with a rotisserie is to balance the food neatly on the spit so that the motor doesn't strain. Many rotisserie kits come with counterweights or other devices that can be used to balance the food. Generally when spit-roasting, choose pieces of meat or poultry that are relatively symmetrical or cylindrical in shape, although I will admit I recently devoured some delicious baby back ribs (not very cylindrical or even symmetrical) that were spitted and roasted over hickory coals.

Gear

When you page through mail order catalogs you see just about every kind of gimcrack and geegaw for the barbecue that you could imagine. You can always find the perfect gadget for the most tech-crazed cook, and if you are looking for a present to encourage somebody to get out there and grill, why, just go for it—buy that chrome-plated velvet-handled digital triple-calibrated corn kernel scraper and electric epazote mincer for $99.99. But most grillers, myself included, use just a couple of tried and true tools, battered and scarred from years of use.

My main tools for the grill are two or three pairs of spring-loaded stainless steel tongs. I own two or three since I keep bringing tongs to barbecues and leaving them, but one is really all I need. I use tongs to put food on, move food around, and take food off the grill. I also use tongs to lift grates and grills, flip up the top of the woodbox to check on smoking chips, and when I want to move hot coals or add more charcoal to the fire. My other tools: an apron with a towel, of course, tucked into my belt (nobody who ever cooked in a restaurant can ever cook without a towel in the belt); an oven mitt or two if the tongs can't lift the grid; an old fireplace poker and ash shovel to move coals around and to poke the fire from time to time; a large spatula to scrape up pieces of fish or meat that stick to the grill; and a brush or mop to brush on sauces, glazes, and mops.

Blender or Food Processor While this isn't strictly speaking grilling gear, a blender or food processor is especially helpful when you grill often. Since many sauces and marinades for grilled foods depend on tomatoes, onions, chiles, and so on, the blender or food processor saves a lot of time and effort. I often use a small stick blender to make sauces or salsas: I soak a dried chile or two in warm water, and grill tomatoes, chiles, and onions. As each ingredient is ready I simple toss it into the small cup that came with the stick blender, puree it coarsely, and pour the puree into a mixing bowl. I give everything a stir, taste for salt and pepper, and serve this quick and delicious salsa with the food I've grilled. Nothing could be simpler, and the salsa has the smoky tang of the grill that I love.

Thermometers I have to confess that one gadget I will never be without is an instant-read meat thermometer. These are inserted into meat or poultry as it cooks and will

give you a reading of the internal temperature in a few seconds. I think the meat thermometer is essential to gauge when meat or poultry is ready to take off the grill. The trick is to remove the food from the heat and let it rest for 5, 10, or even 15 minutes (depending on size or thickness) before you are going to serve it. This gives the heat levels inside the piece of meat or poultry time to equalize and the juices to become evenly distributed. The internal temperature will rise 5°F to 10°F, again depending on the size of the piece of food. For tenderness, succulence, and safety a meat thermometer is an important part of cooking.

Many grills come with built-in thermometers that will tell you the ambient temperature inside the covered grill—very handy for gauging cooking times and doneness; oven thermometers on the unheated portion of the grill can serve the same purpose; or you can insert an instant-read meat thermometer into one of the top vents of a kettle barbecue to check the temperature inside.

Wire or Cellulose Brush Wire brushes with scrapers are made specifically for cleaning barbecue grills. They work well and I have used a number of types over the years. These days I use a cellulose grill brush that seems to do a better job of getting bits of burnt food off the grill and maintaining a lightly oiled surface. From time to time I wipe the cold grill down with a damp cloth or paper towel, empty ashes from the charcoal grill, and clean the grease catcher and metal baffles of the propane grill.

Oil Spray or Brush I think it is essential to clean and oil the grill with every use. This cuts down on food sticking and tearing and makes it easy to turn and move whatever you are cooking. I use vegetable oil spray on the cold grill before I start cooking and often I spray foods like fish or seafood with oil before cooking. You can also use a brush or a piece of paper towel dipped in oil for oiling the grill or food.

Grids and Baskets Some foods are too small or too delicate to put right onto the grill. Green beans, for example, or asparagus or shrimp can fall through the grill and fish can easily stick or break apart. You can find a wide variety of perforated metal grids or baskets that will help with any small or delicate pieces of food you want to

grill. I use a large piece of blackened iron with ¼-inch holes as well as a hinged stainless steel fish basket, but you'll find the right kind of grid or basket for your own style of grilling with a little bit of trial and error.

Safety

Common sense is what is needed for safety in most situations, and especially when you are dealing with fire. If you follow a few rules and exercise reasonable caution, grilling and barbecuing should be as safe as any other type of cooking. Here are some rules to grill by:

- **Never cook with charcoal indoors.** Burning charcoal produces carbon monoxide which is deadly in enclosed spaces. If you use a stovetop grill or gas grill indoors make sure you have an exhaust fan and plenty of ventilation.
- **Set up your grill,** charcoal or gas, on a flat surface and away from flammable materials and overhanging trees. If there are small children around, kid-proof the grill and surrounding areas.
- **If you use starter fluid,** make sure it's stored in a safe area. Never pour lighter fluid onto hot or burning coals. Never use gasoline or other flammable liquids other than commercial lighter fluid. Be careful with electric starters and remove them as soon as the coals ignite.
- **Use only approved fuels** (charcoal, hardwoods, commercial propane tanks, natural gas lines installed by a professional). Don't use leftover lumber or building materials or any softwoods such as pine in the grill. Don't overload the grill and make sure the fire grid and vents are secure and operating properly.
- **When you discard coals or ashes,** be sure that they are cold. Be especially careful when grilling or barbecuing in high-fire areas. Sparks can fly from charcoal (especially the free-form variety) and can ignite surrounding brush and trees. I don't recommend charcoal grills in wilderness regions; use propane or a controlled and permissable campfire.

Ingredients

With the growing interest in American regional and ethnic cooking, more and more of what used to be called exotic ingredients are showing up on supermarket shelves. Chiles, salsas, and other Southwestern ingredients are easy to find in most areas; barbecue sauces and hot pepper sauces are everywhere it seems; and Asian sauces, spices, and produce are widely available. If you can't find an ingredient in your supermarket, head for a Latino or Asian grocery. If you don't have success there, look in Sources, page 200, for mail-order vendors.

Achiote or Annato Seed This lightly pungent reddish-yellow seed is ground into a powder and used to flavor and color Latin American and East Indian foods. Achiote creates a lovely, yellow color in the cooked dish and contributes a pleasant undertone of flavor. Native Americans used achiote as body paint and its main use today is as an organic food coloring.

Asian Chile Oil Often spelled chili oil, this spicy condiment is a common addition to Chinese and other Asian dishes. It is sesame or soy oil flavored with hot Asian chiles, and is usually red in color and quite hot. Sometimes red pepper flakes are left in the oil; be especially careful with these and don't let too many of the flakes get in the dish as they can burn the taste buds easily. I keep my Asian chile oil in the refrigerator to keep it fresh and discard it after a few months. The oil is excellent in marinades in which you want a jolt of heat and a lightly nutty flavor.

Black Beans I don't mean *frijoles negros*, the delicious dried black bean of Cuban and Mexican cooking, but the salted and fermented soy beans used in many dishes by Chinese cooks. I often add black bean and garlic sauce to Asian marinades; hot bean paste, made from black beans flavored with chiles, can be substituted for Asian chile oil in any recipe.

Chili Powder Commercial chili powder (the best that is widely available is Gebhardt) is a blend of dried ground red chiles, oregano, cumin, and garlic powder. Some contain salt, so check the label. I prefer to use pure ground chile powder, available in Latino groceries or by mail order (see Sources, page 200). I particularly like the flavors of ancho, New Mexican, and chipotle chile powders (see Chiles, page 60).

Chipotles en Adobo Chipotles are dried and smoked ripe jalapeño chiles (see Chiles, page 60). They can be purchased in Latino markets in dried form, as chipotle chile powder, and in small (7 ounce) cans packed in a spicy tomato-based adobo sauce. These canned chipotles en adobo are very convenient and can be used in salsas and marinades. The adobo sauce is delicious when smeared over pork, chicken, or fish before grilling.

Five-Spice Powder This is a blend of aromatic spices often used in Chinese cookery. The blend usually includes ground star anise, fennel seeds, cinnamon, cloves, and Szechuan pepper, but can also include other spices such as licorice root and dried ginger. Use whenever you want a subtle, anise flavor. I find five-spice powder is excellent in rubs for chicken or fish. It also adds an interesting undertone to grilled fruits and pastries. Five-spice powder is widely available in the spice sections of most markets, in Asian groceries, and from mail-order sources (see page 200).

Fruit Syrups There are a number of excellent fruit syrups available in supermarkets and specialty stores these days. I use them in sauces for grilled fruit and in marinades and salsas where I want a taste of sweet fruit or berries. Torani, an Italian brand, offers a wide range of flavors including tamarind. Knott's Berry Farm and Smucker's are American producers with flavorful berry and other fruit syrups.

Ginger Fresh ginger can be found in most markets. It contributes spice and a bit of heat to marinades, dressings, and Asian sauces. I often use Japanese pickled ginger, a popular sushi garnish, to flavor and garnish Asian-style dishes and sauces. Dried ground ginger and candied ginger can also be used to add the characteristic snap that ginger provides in pastries and sauces.

Ham Fresh ham is delicious when slowly roasted at low temperatures in a covered barbecue. You can substitute it for pork shoulder in recipes. Smoked ham, usually sold precooked, is also tasty when smoke-roasted in a kettle grill. You don't have to cook this ham, just heat it through, but most ham benefits from the drying effect of the roasting and from the added smoke flavor. Look for ham without water or any other liquid added. Hams from small smokehouses are often sold by mail order (see Sources, page 000) and are especially delicious.

Herbs I grow and use fresh herbs in salads, sauces, herb pastes, braises, and stews. Dried herbs can usually be substituted: Use half as much dried herbs as fresh. Dried herbs, since the water content has been removed, will last longer than fresh herbs and are more suitable for use in dry rubs. Herb-flavored oils are easy to make (see Flavored Oils, page 162) and are also widely available in markets. Use them in salads, sauces, and marinades. Stalks of woody herbs can provide aromatic smoke for grilled fish, meat, or poultry (see Woodsmoke and Herb Smoke for Flavor, page 43).

Hoisin Sauce This sweet, pungent, and spicy Chinese sauce is made from soybeans and flavored with garlic, five-spice powder, and often chiles. I use it in Asian-flavored sauces, marinades, and pastes for grilled meat, chicken, or seafood. It's widely available in most markets and by mail order (see Sources, page 200).

Jalapeños en Escabeche These canned, pickled green, jalapeño chiles (see Chiles, page 60) are a welcome addition to salsas and Southwest-style marinades. They are an excellent condiment in themselves (most canned versions include sliced carrots and onions) and can be chopped and added to tacos and burritos. Canned jalapeños en escabeche can be found in most markets or ordered by mail (see Sources, page 200).

Jícama A bulbous root popular with Mexican and Southwest cooks, jícama adds a delicious crunch to salads and salsas. It can also be served as a tasty appetizer or side dish, sliced with a squeeze of lemon and dusted with chile powder and salt.

Miso A pungent, salty paste made from fermented soybeans, miso is a staple of Japanese cooks who use it in soups and sauces. Miso makes a delicious, tangy base for pastes and marinades for grilled seafood, chicken, pork, or vegetables. It can also be blended with sake or mirin, ginger, wasabi, and other flavorings to make a lively dipping sauce for grilled foods. White miso includes rice paste in the mix and is rather delicate in flavor; yellow and red miso are more intense and pungent. Miso is available in many markets, in Asian specialty stores, and by mail order (see Sources, page 200).

Paprika Made from dried and ground red chiles, paprika ranges from mild or sweet to quite hot. It is the basis for many spice rubs in Cajun and other regional American

traditions. American paprika is a bit bland, so I prefer to use Hungarian or Spanish paprika. Hungarian paprika can be found on many supermarket shelves, in regular and hot versions. Spanish paprika is harder to find, but worth searching for or ordering by mail (see Sources, page 200). Spanish smoked paprika, where the dried chiles are smoked before grinding, is especially delicious. It adds a lightly smoky flavor to rubs and sauces that is irresistible. Spanish paprika comes in *dulce* (sweet), *agrodulce* (bittersweet), and *picante* (hot) verisons.

Plum Sauce Chinese plum sauce is a sweet and pungent sauce based on soybeans. It adds flavor to marinades, dressings, and pastes for grilled pork, chicken, or vegetables. Plum sauce is found in most markets or by mail order (see Sources, page 200).

Salsas Salsa recently overtook ketchup as the most popular American condiment. Salsas are Southwest-style sauces of chopped chiles, tomatoes, onions, herbs, and sometimes fruits. Grilled food, unlike food that is sautéed or braised, usually doesn't create its own sauce or gravy. The popularity of salsas parallels the rise in popularity of grilling, as they are easy to make and can be used to add spice and flavor to grilled meats, seafood, and vegetables. Use homemade or store-bought salsas, as you wish, with grilled foods of all kinds and in recipes.

Salt I use regular table salt in my recipes and rubs, and in relatively small amounts compared to some other cookbook authors and chefs. You could certainly substitute Kosher salt or sea salt, if you wish, but I confess that I am not a salt lover. I have been trying, successfully, to lower my salt intake over the years and my recipes (and taste buds) reflect this. This is why most of my recipes suggest that you taste for salt and add more if you wish. I prefer to start with low salt levels and add more to taste, rather than follow the example of many professional chefs who look for an extra kick from salt (often from some exotic beach on a far-off isle) and often "finish" a dish with a liberal sprinkling of expensive salt before serving. I've come not to like this extra level of salt and I've seen enough gourmet salts marketed at very high prices to be just a bit wary of the claims of the "salt mavens."

Tomatillos Tomatillos, also called ground cherries, are not really tomatoes, but these small, green fruits in papery husks do add texture and flavor to Mexican and Southwest dishes. They are sold fresh or canned and add a tangy undertone to salsas.

Wasabi This is the green paste you find accompanying sushi or sashimi. Similar, though not related, to horseradish, this root is ground to a paste and used to flavor sauces for grilled meats, poultry, or seafood. It is available in the United States as a powder or paste. I find that the powder, mixed to a paste with water and used when freshly prepared is more flavorful than the paste that usually comes in small tubes and can deteriorate over time.

CHILES

Chiles and other peppers are all part of the capsicum family and originated in the New World. They are now a part of many diverse cuisines and add their tangy undertone to everything from Asian green papaya salad to Mexican salsas, Hungarian goulash to Cajun gumbo. Peppers are grown all over the world and range in heat levels from very mild to blazingly hot.

Care should be taken in handling hot chiles (jalapeño and hotter): Remove the stems and seeds and discard; wash your hands thoroughly after handling chiles or wear latex gloves; don't touch your eyes or mouth when you are working with hot chiles; take a little taste of any hot chile before adding it to a dish, as heat levels vary even within types; always add less hot chile to a dish and then taste for heat levels—you can always add more. Do not peel small, hot chiles; grill and peel large green chiles (see Grilled Peppers, page 113). Dried chiles should be reconstituted by soaking in warm water to cover for about 15 minutes; remove and discard the seeds and stems; puree the torn-up chiles with a little of the soaking water or a grilled tomato or two in a blender or food processor before using in salsas or sauces.

Chiles and peppers are available in a number of forms: green or unripe fresh peppers (green bell peppers, poblano, Anaheim chiles); ripe fresh peppers (red or yellow bell peppers, ripe jalapeños); canned green or red peppers (whole or chopped, fresh or pickled); dried ripe peppers (ancho, pasilla, Spanish choricero); dried smoked red peppers (chipotles); pure ground dried peppers (ancho, New Mexican); ground smoked dried peppers (chipotle powder, Spanish smoked paprika); blended ground dried peppers (paprika, commercial chili powder). Chiles are also used to make many types of commercial bottled hot sauces; a few of my favorites are Tabasco, Crystal, Tapatio, and Bufalo. The best place to find most chiles, powders, and sauces is a Latino market, or see Sources (page 200).

Here is a list of the more common chiles and peppers, starting with the mildest and ending with the hottest:

Bell peppers are large, sweet peppers sold fresh in most American markets. Green peppers are unripe; red, yellow, chocolate, purple, and other bell peppers are ripe. Use, peeled or unpeeled, in salads, sauces, or any dish where you want a mild, herbaceous flavor. Very tasty grilled, peeled, and sliced, tossed with a vinaigrette.

Anaheim chiles are large green or red chiles that are widely available and provide a mild, tangy flavor in salsas and salads. Like most green chiles, Anaheims are best grilled and peeled (see Grilled Peppers, page 113). Mild green chiles are available fire-roasted, peeled, and canned, whole or chopped. Ortega makes good canned green chiles that can be substituted in recipes calling for fresh green chiles.

Poblano chiles are large green chiles with a pleasant, mildly spicy character. Grill and peel like Anaheims. When ripe and dried, poblanos are called anchos, which are also made into pure chile powders. Ancho is my favorite chile powder and the one I used in most recipes in this book. You can substitute New Mexican or other chile powder in all recipes.

New Mexican chiles are sold both green and red as fresh chiles and often as a dried red chile in *ristras*, the long strings of chiles you see hanging from the eaves of Southwestern houses. New Mexican chile powder is a bit hot, with a pleasant taste and texture.

Chili powder is the name given to the standard blend you find on supermarket shelves. This is usually a mildly hot mix of various dried red chiles blended with herbs (most often oregano and cumin), garlic powder, and sometimes salt. Check the label for salt and be careful when using in recipes. Gebhardt makes a good commercial chili powder.

Pasilla is a medium-hot chile, usually sold dried, but occasionally found as a fresh green chile. The powder is mildly hot with a pleasantly sweet undertone.

Choricero is a Spanish dried red chile with a medium-hot, nutty flavor.

Jalapeño is our most popular hot chile and is usually sold fresh and green, although you can sometimes find fresh red jalapeños. Dried red jalapeños are often smoked and called chipotles. These are available dried or canned with adobo sauce. Green jalapeños are also sold canned and pickled or en escabeche.

Cayenne pepper is made from ground dried red cayenne chiles, extremely hot small chiles that are occasionally found dried.

Chile de arbol is a small hot chile, usually sold dried.

Serrano is a small, cylindrical green chile that is quite hot and provides a tangy acidic flavor in salsas. As with other fresh hot chiles, do not peel; remove seeds and stems to lower the heat level, if you wish.

Habanero is the hottest chile that is widely available. This stubby yellow chile is also called the Scotch bonnet chile in the Caribbean. Be very careful with habenero chiles; they are so hot that they really burn the taste buds and should be used sparingly, if at all.

Fish & Seafood

Seafood and fish are at their best when grilled briefly on a hot fire. The idea is simple: Get the fire good and hot (mesquite charcoal is my favorite fuel for grilling fish and seafood since it burns at such a high temperature), oil the fish or seafood to keep it from sticking to the grill (or put it in an oiled grill basket if the fish is very delicate or if the pieces of fish or seafood are small), and cook until just barely done. The overarching rule is not to overcook anything from the sea—think sushi.

I like to season seafood and fish lightly with a spicy dry rub, herb paste, or flavored butter. The flavors of lemon, lime, and garlic go well with most seafood, and Japanese and other Asian chefs often pair the lively flavors of soy, miso, and wasabi with fish. Go lightly with seasonings, however, as you don't want to overpower the delicate flavors of seafood.

THE CLAMBAKE

A popular way of barbecuing that dates from the early colonial days and seems to define outdoor cooking in New England and along the East Coast is the clambake. In these regions clams, lobsters, and ears of corn are steamed under seaweed on driftwood fires while chicken, burgers, and often steaks and sausages are grilled over coals. When I was a kid my family had clambakes and outdoor barbecues at Sheepshead Bay on Long Island. During these events, which were often part of events put on by local unions, police, and other organizations, I would watch my dad, uncles, and family friends build huge fires and roast clams and lobsters under seaweed and burlap covers. After they raked off the seaweed and piled the clams, lobsters, and corn on plank tables, they'd grill chicken and steak for the grownups, and hot dogs and burgers for hordes of hungry kids. Potato salad, coleslaw, beer, iced tea, and huge pans of peach cobbler with homemade ice cream rounded off the feast. Whenever my sisters and I reminisce about the clambakes, we recall that even the sand tasted good—and of course everything gets even better with each retelling.

Follow the same rule with the smoke and use a lightly aromatic wood such as mesquite or alder, or a fruitwood such as apple or cherry with seafood and fish, rather than more powerful woods such as hickory or oak.

Large prawns or shrimp are ideal for grilling. Some prefer to leave the shells on while grilling to protect the tender flesh, but I prefer to let my seasonings get into the flesh of the shellfish and not just on the shells. Use large prawns or langoustines, if you can find them, as they are easier to handle and won't fall through the grill. If you are grilling smaller shrimp, use a perforated grid or grill basket. Scallops are delicious grilled, and make sure to buy the largest and freshest ones you can find. Large sea scallops can be cooked right on an oiled grill; smaller scallops should be skewered (two skewers stabilize seafood better than one) or place them on an oiled perforated grid or into a grill basket.

Lobster always makes a dramatic presentation. I often grill West Coast spiny lobster, and I have eaten it many times with fresh salsa in Baja California, and Mexican seafood grill restaurants. East Coast lobster, with its large, meaty claws, is also excellent on the grill and is best served with the traditional accompaniment of drawn or melted butter and herbs. Crab—Pacific Dungeness, Atlantic blue crab, and Alaska king crab—are also good choices for the grill.

Cooking oysters, clams, and mussels on the grill is actually quite easy. You simply need to scrub the shellfish, put them directly on a grill over high heat, cover and cook them until their shells open. Remove the top shell, and spoon in some salsa, aïoli, or your favorite spicy sauce. Discard any shellfish whose shells don't open.

Most fish can be grilled with good results, although I would avoid delicate fillets such as sole. These can often break up, even in a grill basket, and fall into the fire. Choose firm-fleshed fish in pieces at least ¾-inch thick. Ahi tuna is one of the best fish for grilling. Its firm red flesh has a meaty flavor and care should be taken not to over-cook it. Ahi tuna is best served rare (it is often used for sashimi) with just the surfaces seared and grill-marked. Halibut, swordfish, shark, or escolar are all firm white-fleshed fish that are delicious when grilled to the medium-rare stage. I especially like escolar, a Hawaiian fish available in West Coast markets, that has a high oil content and really sizzles when it hits the grill. Salmon is wonderful when grilled directly (steaks or small fillets) or smoke-roasted (large fillets or whole fish) in a kettle grill. Salmon takes well to light smoking—Native Americans of the Northwest often roast it, pegged to cedar planks beside alder fires. Whole fish, small or large, can be either grilled directly or roasted by indirect cooking in kettle grills. Extra care must be used when cooking a whole fish so that you don't end up with a lot of small pieces. I use a hinged grill basket to keep the fish from breaking up when turning or removing from the grill.

Gulf Coast Prawns with Lemon and Sweet Pepper Relish

SERVES 6 AS A FIRST COURSE, 4 AS A MAIN COURSE

Lemon and peppers accentuate the rich yet delicate flavors of Gulf Coast prawns, and grilling is the best way to cook these succulent shellfish. I shell the prawns to let the flavors of the spice rub penetrate, but if you prefer you can leave the shells on, peel them yourself, and lick your fingers as you eat. The spice rub will keep, covered in a jar, for a few months. It is also delicious on scallops or any kind of grilled seafood.

Lemon-Garlic Spice Rub

2 tablespoons sweet Hungarian or Spanish paprika

2 tablespoons garlic powder

1 tablespoon chile powder

1 tablespoon lemon pepper

1 teaspoon dried tarragon

½ teaspoon cayenne or more to taste

½ tablespoon salt

24 large prawns, shelled and deveined

Lemon and Sweet Pepper Relish

1 red bell pepper

1 yellow bell pepper

1 large red onion

2 lemons

1 tablespoon sweet sherry

2 tablespoons olive oil

Salt and pepper to taste

Make the spice rub: Mix the ingredients together in a small bowl. Rub generously over the prawns. Reserve leftover spice rub for another use.

Prepare the grill for direct cooking over very high heat (400°F to 450°F). Brush or spray the grill with oil.

Make the Lemon and Sweet Pepper Relish: Grill the peppers whole over high heat, turning often, until charred on all sides. Remove from the grill and place in a plastic bag for 5 to 10 minutes. Cut the onion into ½-inch-thick slices. Grill over high heat for 2 to 3 minutes per side and remove from the heat. Peel, remove and discard the stems and seeds, and coarsely chop the peppers. Chop the onions coarsely. Add the peppers and onions to a bowl. Juice 1 of the lemons and whisk the juice together with the sherry and oil. Slice the other lemon thinly and set aside for garnish. Toss the peppers and onions with the dressing and add salt and pepper to taste.

Grill the prawns for 2 to 3 minutes per side over high heat until they are pink and firm, but still juicy. Arrange the peppers and onions on a platter, place the prawns on top, and garnish with the sliced lemons. A tart Sauvignon Blanc from California would make a nice match.

Miso-Crusted Scallops with Grilled Baby Bok Choy

SERVES 6 AS A FIRST COURSE, 4 AS A MAIN COURSE

Miso-Wasabi Marinade

1 cup white miso (see Ingredients, page 54)

¼ cup mirin or sake

2 tablespoons tamari or soy sauce

1 tablespoon or more wasabi paste (see Ingredients, page 54)

24 large sea scallops

8 heads baby bok choy

Soy-Garlic Marinade

1 cup shoyu or Japanese soy sauce

¼ cup peanut or other vegetable oil

2 cloves garlic, minced

2 tablespoons sweet sherry

Miso is a flavorful Japanese soybean paste that adds a salty tang to soups, sauces, and marinades. It comes in white, yellow, and red versions. I prefer to use the more delicate white miso, but any type will do here. Wasabi, a spicy Japanese condiment, is available as a paste or powder. Follow the directions on the package for reconstituting the powder. Both the Miso-Wasabi Marinade and the Soy-Garlic Marinade are also delicious with grilled black cod, salmon, escolar, tuna, or other fish as well as chicken or pork.

Make the Miso-Wasabi Marinade: Mix together the miso, mirin, tamari, and the wasabi paste in a small bowl. Add more wasabi, if you want a higher heat level. Brush both sides of the scallops generously with the miso marinade. Set the leftover marinade aside. Split the bok choy in half lengthwise. Mix together the shoyu, oil, garlic, and sherry in a flat bowl and place the pieces of bok choy cut side down in the mixture. Let the scallops and bok choy marinate at room temperature for up to 1 hour.

Prepare the grill for direct cooking over very high heat (400°F to 450°F). Brush or spray the grill with oil. If using a grill basket or perforated grid, brush or spray it with oil. Use a grill basket or perforated grid if the scallops look like they might fall through the grill, or skewer the scallops.

Grill the scallops over direct heat, grill for 2 to 3 minutes per side, or until they are opaque and firm to the touch. Remove from the grill and brush with a little more of the miso marinade.

Remove the bok choy from the marinade, reserving the excess marinade. Place the bok choy on the grill, cut side down, over high heat. Grill for 2 or 3 minutes per side, basting with the shoyu mixture occasionally. Remove to a platter with the scallops.

Whisk the reserved miso marinade and soy-garlic marinade together to make a dipping sauce for the scallops. Serve with steamed rice and dry sake or New York Riesling.

Catfish Fillets with Grilled Corn Chow-Chow

SERVES 4

Grilled Corn Chow-Chow

2 cups grilled corn kernels (see page 191) or cooked fresh or frozen corn kernels

2 cups shredded cabbage

1 red bell pepper, seeded and finely chopped

1 jalapeño chile, seeded and finely chopped

1 onion, finely chopped

½ cup white vinegar

½ cup vegetable oil

2 tablespoons sugar

2 tablespoons pickling spice, tied into a cheesecloth bag

½ teaspoon or more red pepper flakes

½ cup chopped green onions

Salt, pepper, and Tabasco or other hot sauce to taste

Spicy Rub

2 tablespoons sweet Hungarian or Spanish paprika

1 tablespoon hot Hungarian or Spanish paprika

¼ teaspoon or more cayenne

1 tablespoon garlic powder

1 tablespoon onion powder

1 tablespoon dried marjoram

1 tablespoon celery salt

8 catfish fillets or other white-fleshed fish fillets

Catfish is a delicate white fish that is often featured at fish fries and served breaded and fried on sandwiches all through the Midwest and South. It is also delicious when seasoned with a spice rub and grilled, although care must be taken not to overcook catfish. An oiled grill basket is recommended here to keep the fillets intact and for easy turning. Chow-chow, piccalilli, pickled corn relish, sweet and sour watermelon rinds, and countless relishes and pickles have added spice and lively flavors to American farm tables from our earliest days to the present. You can use leftover grilled corn here or grill the corn following the directions on page 191, or use fresh-cut or frozen corn if you wish, in the recipe below and other recipes calling for grilled corn.

Make the Grilled Corn Chow-Chow: In a large bowl, mix together the corn, cabbage, bell pepper, chile, and onion. In a nonreactive saucepan, combine the vinegar, oil, sugar, pickling spice, and red pepper flakes and bring to a boil. Reduce the heat, and simmer for 10 minutes, stirring occasionally. Remove the spice bag and pour the hot dressing over the vegetables. Let sit at room temperature for 2 hours. Stir in the green onions and taste for salt, pepper, and Tabasco.

Prepare the grill for direct cooking over very high heat (400°F to 450°F). Brush or spray the grill or grill basket with oil.

Make the Spicy Rub: In a small bowl, mix all the ingredients together. Sprinkle both sides of the catfish fillets with the spice rub. Use an oiled grill basket for any delicate fish such as catfish. Grill the fish for 2 minutes or more per side until firm. Do not overcook.

Serve the fillets with the Grilled Corn Chow-Chow and Grilled Summer Squash with Fresh Herb Marinade (page 179). Iced tea with lemon or a Coke with a wedge of lemon would go well.

Swordfish Steaks with Lime-Ginger Pickled Onions and Papaya Vinaigrette

Swordfish is at its best when grilled. The firm texture and almost meaty flavor seems to be accentuated when the steaks are grilled quickly over a hot fire. Escolar, a Hawaiian fish with a high oil content, is another of my favorite fish on the grill. Either can be used in this recipe; shark, halibut, or other firm-fleshed white fish are also good. Use sweet onions when you can find them for the Lime-Ginger Pickled Onions, or substitute large red or yellow onions. Pickled ginger, often used as a garnish for sushi, is available in most markets today (see Ingredients, page 54).

Lemon Garlic Spice Rub (see page 000)

Lime-Ginger Pickled Onions

1 large sweet onion (Maui, Walla Walla, Vidalia)

1 teaspoon salt

Juice of 1 lime

1 tablespoon chopped pickled ginger (see page 200)

1 tablespoon chopped fresh ginger

Papaya Vinaigrette

2 papayas

½ sweet onion (Maui, Vidalia, Walla Walla)

¼ cup rice vinegar

1 tablespoon Dijon mustard

Juice of 1 lemon

1 cup peanut or other vegetable oil

Salt and pepper to taste

4 swordfish or escolar steaks, at least 1 inch thick

Vegetable oil or oil spray

Make the Lime-Ginger Pickled Onions: Peel and slice the onion very thinly. In a bowl, combine the onion with the salt, lime juice, and pickled and fresh ginger and let sit at room temperature for up to 1 hour.

Make the vinaigrette: Peel, seed, and dice the papayas. Put all the vinaigrette ingredients except the oil and salt and pepper in a blender or food processor and pulse to combine. With the blender or processor running, gradually add the oil to emulsify. Pour into a bowl and taste for salt and pepper.

Trim the swordfish or escolar of any bones and brush or spray with oil. Sprinkle both sides generously with Lemon-Garlic Spice Rub. Let sit at room temperature for up to 1 hour.

Prepare the grill for direct cooking over high heat (375°F to 400°F). Brush or spray the grill with oil.

Place the fish on the grill over high heat and cook for 3 to 4 minutes per side, until the surface is lightly browned and grill-marked. Swordfish or escolar should be firm to the touch and cooked through, opaque but still juicy in the center.

Drizzle the vinaigrette on swordfish or escolar steaks and around the serving plate. Garnish with the pickled onions and serve with Grilled Summer Squash with Fresh Herb Marinade (page 179) and a Sauvignon Blanc from New Zealand or France's Loire Valley.

Oysters on the Grill with Three-Chile Salsa

SERVES 6 AS A FIRST COURSE, 4 AS A MAIN COURSE

While oysters are always tasty raw on the half shell or in a savory stew, my favorite way to eat these briny bivalves is right off the grill, topped with a spicy salsa. When barbecuing oysters, I prefer big, deep-shelled varieties that have plenty of juice and meat, such as Pacific or Kumamoto oysters. Ask your seafood purveyor about local varieties. As with all seafood, of course, the fresher the better. Discard any oysters that smell fishy or don't open when heated on the grill. This salsa features different kinds of chiles with varying heat levels and flavors. Feel free to change the types of chiles or amounts to your tastes. Be careful when handling chiles. Always wash your hands afterward or use plastic gloves and don't touch your eyes when peeling, seeding, or chopping hot chiles. See Chiles, page 60, for more information about chiles and how to handle them.

Three-Chile Salsa

1 Anaheim, chilaca, poblano, or other large green chile, grilled and peeled (see page 60)

1 jalapeño chile, seeded

1 serrano chile, seeded, or more to taste

1 onion

2 red tomatoes

2 yellow tomatoes

½ cup coarsely chopped cilantro

Juice of 1 lime or lemon

Salt to taste

48 oysters, scrubbed and debearded

Prepare the grill for direct cooking over medium-high heat (350°F).

Finely chop the chiles, onion, and tomatoes by hand or using a food processor. Stir together in a bowl with the cilantro and lemon juice and taste for salt. If you like a hotter sauce, add more chopped serrano chile.

Place the oysters in the shells, deep side down, directly over medium-high heat and cover the grill. Cook until the shells open, usually in about 7 to 8 minutes, depending on the size of the oysters and the heat level. As the oysters open, carefully remove them to a platter, keeping as much of the juice in the shell as you can. Using a glove or oven mitt, twist off the top shells and discard; spoon salsa on top of the oysters. Discard any unopened oysters. Serve immediately, with Mexican beer with wedges of lime.

Ahi Tuna with Lemon-Wasabi Marinade and Mango-Mint Salsa

SERVES 4

4 ahi tuna steaks, at least 1 inch thick

Lemon-Wasabi Marinade

4 tablespoons wasabi paste

2 tablespoons tamari or soy sauce

2 tablespoons mirin or sake

Juice of 1 lemon

Lemon pepper

Mango-Mint Salsa

3 cups chopped mango

1 cup chopped fresh mint

1 jalapeño chile, seeded and finely chopped (see page 60)

2 tablespoons finely chopped or grated ginger

1 tablespoon rice vinegar

Juice of 2 limes

1 tablespoon sesame oil

2 tablespoons peanut or other vegetable oil

1 tablespoon tamari or soy sauce

Use only the freshest, sashimi-grade tuna here. Red-fleshed ahi is a favorite on the grill, but other types of tuna such as yellowtail or albacore are also delicious. Be sure not to overcook tuna. It is best served rare, since it dries out when overcooked. The Lemon-Wasabi Marinade can also be used with grilled swordfish, shark, halibut, or escolar. For information about Asian ingredients see Ingredients, page 54.

Trim the tuna of any skin and bone.

Make the marinade: mix together the wasabi, tamari, mirin, and lemon juice. Brush both sides of the fish with the marinade. Sprinkle both sides of the tuna with lemon pepper. Let the tuna marinate at room temperature for up to an hour.

Make the Mango-Mint Salsa: In a serving bowl, mix together the mango, mint, chile, and ginger. In a small bowl, whisk together the rice vinegar, lime juice, oils, and tamari. Toss the mango and mint with the dressing.

Prepare the grill for direct cooking over very high heat (400°F to 450°F). Brush or spray the grill with oil.

Grill the tuna over the highest heat possible for 2 to 3 minutes per side, until the surface is grill-marked but the center is still rare. Do not overcook.

Serve the tuna with the salsa and sake or a buttery California Chardonnay.

Whole Grilled Fish

Grilling a whole fish may seem daunting at first, but with a few grill tricks and some care, it's a technique that produces deliciously tasty fish and a dramatic presentation at the table. The main trick is to prepare the grill well and to be gentle handling the fish during cooking. A grill basket is an excellent investment, if you intend to grill whole fish often. These come in varying sizes and shapes and make turning fish and getting them on and off the grill an easy task. Another important consideration in grilling fish is size: Small and medium fish (up to 5 pounds) such as trout, pompano, striped bass, or mackerel should be cooked on direct heat; large whole fish like salmon or large salmon fillets or other big pieces of fish are best cooked by indirect heat. Smoking whole or large pieces of fish on the grill is another way to prepare salmon or other oily fish in a kettle grill, water smoker, or offset smoker-cooker. Determining when fish is done requires a bit of judgment: Most fish tastes best at the medium-rare stage (135°F) with the center just turning opaque, the flesh firm and beginning to flake; some fish like tuna and salmon are tastier rare (120°F to 125°F), with the center still uncooked and the outer flesh opaque. Use a thermometer on thicker pieces of fish and test smaller pieces by cutting into the fish with a thin, sharp knife.

Method I: Grilling Small to Medium Fish

SERVES 4

Use this technique for whole fish up to about 5 pounds: trout, pompano or yellowtail, small striped bass and sea bass, freshwater largemouth and smallmouth bass, large freshwater sunfish or crappies, and small ocean perch, groupers, and steelhead. Gut and scale the fish and remove large fins.

2 to 4 small to medium whole fish
Lemons
Onion
Fennel leaves, tarragon, parsley, or other fresh herbs
Olive oil
Salt and pepper

Prepare the grill for direct cooking over medium-high heat (350°F). Add alder, mesquite, or other hardwood chips or chunks if you wish, following the directions on page 43. Brush or spray the grill basket or grill with oil.

Rinse the fish inside and out under cold running water. Rub inside and out with lemon juice and put a few lemon slices in the cavity. Thinly slice the onion and put a few slices in the cavity. Reserving a few sprigs for garnish, chop the herbs and put a handful in the cavity. Rub the outside of the fish with oil and sprinkle with salt and pepper.

Put the fish in an oiled grill basket or directly on the grill over the heat. For small fish such as trout, grill for 3 to 5 minutes per side, turning carefully once, until the skin is grill-marked and browning and the flesh is beginning to flake. For medium fish such as pompano or small striped bass, grill for 8 to 10 minutes per side, turning carefully once, until grill-marked and browning and the flesh is beginning to flake. Serve immediately, garnished with sliced lemon and herb sprigs.

Method II:
Grilling Large Fish

SERVES 8 TO 10 AS MAIN COURSE, PLENTY OF HUNGRY FOLKS AT A BUFFET OR PARTY

A whole or half salmon or a large striped bass, sea bass, grouper, or other large whole fish or piece of fish is best cooked using indirect heat. There is no need for a drip pan. I find that placing a piece of oiled heavy-duty foil under the fish helps in moving the fish off the grill when it is done. (I often just roll the fish onto a platter angled against the grill, using the foil as leverage.) There is no need to turn the fish here. It will be fully cooked by roasting in the indirect heat and will pick up plenty of flavor from the wood smoke. The Canadian Fishery rule is a handy rule of thumb in cooking large fish: They say that you should cook fish by any method for 10 minutes per inch of thickness, measured at the thickest part. In my opinion this is a bit too long, but the idea is a good one. I start checking with a thermometer and a sharp knife in the center of the fish after 5 minutes to the inch, measured at the thickest part. I take a whole salmon off the grill at 125°F and let it rest for 5 minutes or so before serving. Some might prefer the salmon rarer (120°F) and some medium-rare (135°F). Other fish such as bass and grouper are best cooked to the medium-rare stage (135°F), opaque at the center with the flesh beginning to flake.

1 large whole fish or piece of fish, 5 pounds or more

Lemons

Onion

Fennel leaves, tarragon, parsley, or other fresh herbs

Olive oil

Salt and pepper

Prepare the grill for indirect cooking over medium-high heat (350°F). Add alder, mesquite, or other hardwood chips or chunks if you wish, following the directions on page 43. If you are not using a grill basket, brush or spray the grill with oil or oil a piece of heavy-duty foil and place it on the grill.

Rinse the fish inside and out under cold running water. If using a whole fish, rub inside and out with lemon juice and put a few lemon slices in the cavity. Thinly slice the onion and put a few slices in the cavity. Reserving a few sprigs for garnish, chop the herbs and put a handful in the cavity. Rub the outside of the fish with oil and sprinkle with salt and pepper. If you are cooking a large fillet by this method, rub both sides with lemon juice and olive oil, and sprinkle with salt and pepper. Place onion and lemon slices on top of the fish; remove and discard if they start to char or burn during cooking.

Put the fish in an oiled grill basket, on an oiled piece of heavy-duty foil, or directly on the grill on the unheated portion of the grill. Cover the grill and roast the fish until done, without turning. When the fish is done will depend on its size and thickness and the heat of the fire. Start testing after 30 minutes for most large fish or use the 5-minute-per-inch rule as a rough guide. Remove the fish from the grill and let rest for 5 minutes. Serve, garnished with sliced lemon and herbs.

Grilled Lobster with Garlic and Tarragon Butter

SERVES 4

4 whole lobsters or 8 lobster tails

Garlic and Tarragon Butter

½ pound salted butter

4 cloves garlic, minced

2 tablespoons chopped fresh tarragon or
    1 tablespoon dried

Juice of 1 lemon

Dash of Tabasco or other hot sauce, or
    more to taste

Use either eastern lobster with claws or the Pacific spiny lobster, which has most of its meat in the tail. You could also use fresh or frozen lobster tails with good results. Scampi, langoustines, and large prawns are also delicious grilled with Garlic and Tarragon Butter (follow directions for grilled prawns on page 67). I use tarragon here, but you could substitute virtually any fresh herb such as basil, oregano, or thyme in the flavored butter. Any leftover seafood and herb butter (not very likely in my house with this luscious dish) can be tossed with cooked pasta for a first course or main course (see Pastas, page 97).

Prepare the grill for direct cooking over high heat (375°F to 400°F). Brush or spray the grill with oil.

Kill the lobsters by cutting behind the head with a sharp knife or dropping them into boiling water for 1 to 2 minutes. Using a sharp, heavy knife or cleaver, split the lobsters or lobster tails in half lengthwise through the belly. If there are claws, crack them lightly with the back of the knife or cleaver.

Make the Garlic and Tarragon Butter: In a saucepan over medium heat, melt the butter. Stir in the remaining ingredients and remove from the heat.

Brush the cut side of the lobsters with the tarragon butter. Put the lobsters on the grill, cut side down, and cook for 6 to 7 minutes over direct heat. Move to a cooler part of the grill if flare-ups occur. Turn, baste the lobster meat liberally with the butter, and grill for another 6 to 7 minutes, basting occasionally, until the flesh is firm and opaque. Serve with any remaining butter and a full-bodied Chardonnay or a Pilsner-style lager.

Smoked Salmon

To smoke salmon or other large fish, use a water smoker, an offset smoker-cooker, or a kettle barbecue, and keep heat at low temperatures while you slowly cook the fish in wood smoke. Use alder, apple, hickory, or another aromatic hardwood for the smoke. Brining the fish keeps it moist while it smokes and cooks. Use the recipe below or any one of the many commercial brines or cures available (see Sources, page 200).

Brine for Smoking Fish

¾ cup kosher salt

¼ cup sugar

¼ cup maple syrup

2 tablespoon finely minced ginger

2 tablespoons finely minced garlic

2 tablespoons dehydrated onion flakes

3 or 4 sprigs rosemary

3 or 4 sprigs thyme

12 to 14 black peppercorns

1 cup of dry white wine

1 (4- to 5-pound) fillet of salmon (1 whole side)

Make the brine: Pour 4 cups lukewarm water into a nonreactive container, add the salt and sugar, and stir until dissolved. Stir in the maple syrup. Add the remaining brine ingredients, stir well, and let the mixture cool. If you are serving the salmon fillet to a large group of people, keep it whole, as this makes for a wonderful presentation. If individual portions are desired, cut the salmon into 2- to 4-inch sections. When the brine has cooled completely, place the salmon in the brine, making certain that it is completely covered. Cover the container and place it in the refrigerator overnight or for at least 8 hours. Take the salmon out of the mixture 2 hours before smoking. Pat the fish dry and let it air-dry on a sheet of aluminum foil.

Prepare a low fire (250°F) in a water smoker following the manufacturer's directions and page 47. Add hardwood chips or chunks following the directions on page 43. If using an offset smoker, start 12 to 16 charcoal briquettes in the fire-box. When the coals are gray, spread them into a single layer and add hardwood chunks or chips, enough to bring the temperature of the smoker to 250°F. In a kettle barbecue build a low fire and try to keep the temperature below 300°F.

Smoke roast the salmon for an 1½ to 2 hours, depending on the thickness of the fillet and the heat levels. The salmon should be firm to the touch and will flake easily when it is done. Serve the salmon with a sliced baguette or crackers and sour cream along with thinly sliced sweet or red onions and capers.

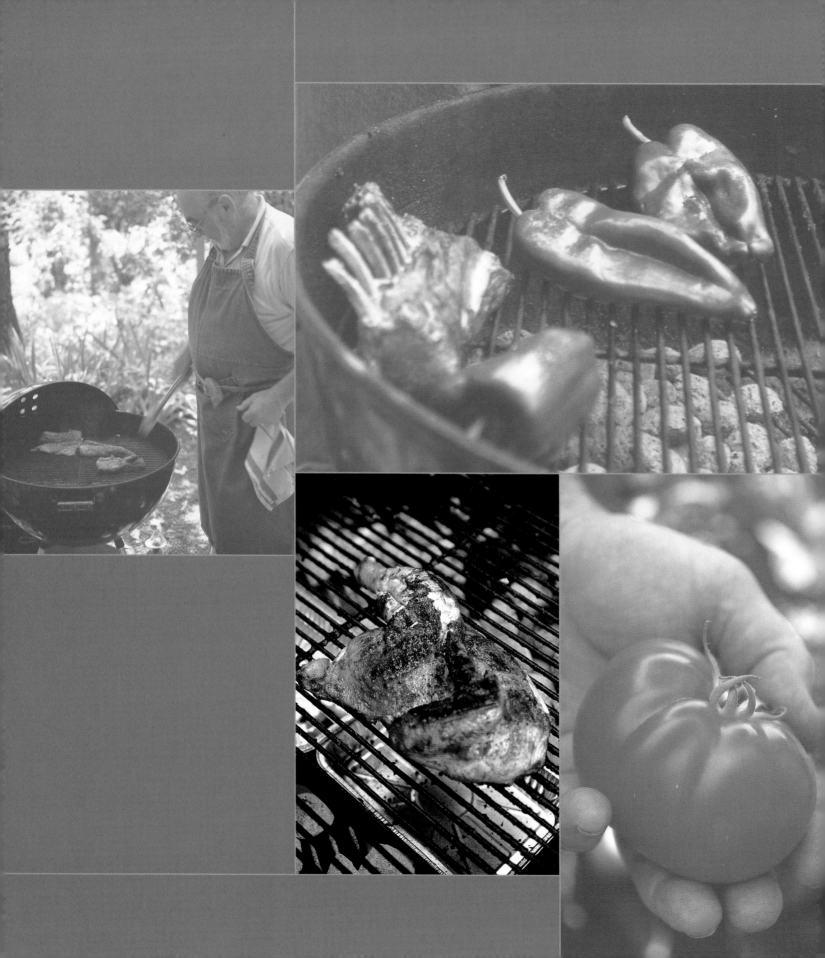

Birds

Poultry of all types, sizes, and shapes can be cooked with excellent results on the backyard kettle grill. Smaller pieces of chicken, boneless thighs and breasts, for example, are easily cooked on direct heat. I like to season these with a lightly spicy rub, brush or spray the pieces with oil, and grill them over a medium-hot fire until done. These, like all chicken, should be cooked through for safety, to about 160°F, although chicken breasts can be removed at 155°F and allowed to rest for a few minutes for internal temperatures to rise. Larger pieces of chicken, bone-in thighs or breasts, quarters, or halves, should be cooked by the combination grilling-roasting method, in which the food is seared over direct heat and then cooked over indirect heat in a covered grill until done. Whole chickens are best cooked by indirect heat over a drip pan or on a rotisserie, although small

LEFTOVERS

Whenever I fire up the grill, I always cook more than my family or guests can eat. After all, if you are roasting one chicken, why not roast two or three, as they use the same amount of fuel and time. And I don't think of the extra food that I take off the grill as leftovers as in "Are we having leftovers again?" To me, what I put in the refrigerator after a session of grilling provides opportunities for even more delicious meals.

Let's think about that extra smoke-roasted chicken or two I just mentioned. I might use the lightly smoked white meat from the breast on a bed of romaine leaves with sliced fresh tomatoes and Lemon-Pickled Onions (see page 118) for a delicious chicken salad; I'll then cut the dark meat from the legs and thighs and mix it with salsa and some cooked beans for tacos or burritos for another meal. Steak is one grilling favorite I always like to have plenty of in the refrigerator. I'll slice it thinly and put it on shredded Napa cabbage with a tangy chile-basil dressing for Thai-style beef salad, mix it with salsa for carne asada tacos, or combine finely chopped grilled steak with smoke-roasted potatoes, grilled onions, and some spicy barbecue sauce to make a quick steak and potato hash for Sunday brunch.

Grilled vegetables go into salads and on pasta, grilled fish or seafood make seafood cocktails or salads, any cooked pork is likely to end up in barbecue sandwiches or in a casserole with sweet potatoes, apples, and onions. The list goes on; the opportunities are endless. All you need is your grill, plenty of good ingredients, and your imagination and taste buds. When you grill on Sunday evening, grill plenty of whatever you're making, and enjoy it the rest of the week.

chickens, poussins, and Cornish game hens can be split and grilled by the combination grilling-roasting method.

The trick to cooking chicken is to make sure that the interior is done and the exterior is lightly browned, but not charred. For this reason, avoid using a sweet barbecue sauce on the chicken throughout cooking (brush sauce on for the last few minutes only or serve it at the table); cook chicken in a covered grill to get the benefits of roasting. Chicken's rather bland taste is vastly improved by spice and herb rubs, garlic and herb pastes, and marinades. My favorite wood for chicken is oak, although mesquite, alder, and apple also add lightly smoky notes.

Duck is also delicious on the grill. Most domestic duck has a layer of fat underneath the skin, and this can cause flare-ups if the fire is too hot. The best way to grill duck breast is to poke holes in the skin with the tip of a sharp knife and cook it over medium heat to render out the fat. Whole duck is best roasted in a kettle grill at medium-low heat until the skin is crisp and the meat is cooked through. Duck's rich and savory flavors take well to sweet and sour glazes and fruits. Use a mild wood smoke, such as cherry, apple, or alder.

My favorite way to cook a whole turkey is to season it with a savory herb rub and roast it in a smoky kettle grill. I don't usually stuff whole turkey with a traditional stuffing when I smoke-roast it; I prefer to put aromatics such as onion, celery, citrus, garlic, and herbs in the cavity, and bake the stuffing separately on the unheated portion of the grill or in the oven. A small turkey can be cooked successfully on a rotisserie, although care should be taken to balance it carefully on the spit. Turkey parts, breasts and thighs, bone-in or boneless, are delicious when cooked by the combination grilling-roasting method. Thighs are especially good when boned and stuffed with chiles, cheese, or other savory dressings.

Game birds are also good when grilled. Most game is relatively fatless, however, so using an oil-based marinade or wrapping the bird in bacon or pancetta is a good idea. The key here is to prevent the bird from drying out and the flesh becoming tough through overcooking. Wild duck breast, squab, quail, and other small birds can be cooked by combination grilling-roasting; larger birds such as pheasant, guinea hen, and wild turkey should be cooked by indirect roasting. Spice and smoke are welcome additives to wild game. Juniper berries, ginger, and various peppers add lively flavors, and fruits such as currants and raisins are often used in sauces. Hickory and pecan are my preferred woods.

Chicken Breasts with Basil-Garlic Paste and Grilled Green Beans

SERVES 4

Basil-Garlic Paste

½ cup chopped fresh basil or ¼ cup dried

3 cloves garlic, finely chopped

1 teaspoon salt

½ teaspoon black pepper

Olive oil

4 chicken breasts, bone-in, skin-on, or boneless, skinless

Basil-Garlic Oil

1 cup olive oil

½ cup whole basil leaves or ¼ cup dried

Juice of ½ lemon

1 teaspoon salt

½ teaspoon pepper

1 pound fresh green beans

1 pound cherry tomatoes, halved

Whole basil leaves

Salt and pepper to taste

This dish is best made in midsummer when fresh basil is abundant in the garden and at farmer's markets, but you can make do with dried basil any time of year. This herb and garlic paste is infinitely variable: rosemary, thyme, and sage, and you could use just about any fresh herb you wish. Herb oils made in a blender or food processor are wonderful additions to grilled vegetables, pastas, and salads. When grilling green beans, as with most vegetables, less is best. Do not overcook. Use a grill basket or perforated grid to keep beans from falling through the grill.

Make the Basil-Garlic Paste: In a blender, food processor, or mortar, mash the basil, garlic, salt, and pepper together, and stir in just enough oil to make a paste. Smear the paste all over the chicken breasts and refrigerate, tightly wrapped, for up to 12 hours or let sit at room temperature for up to 1 hour. Bring the chicken to room temperature before grilling.

Prepare the grill for combination grilling-roasting at medium-high heat (350°F). Add hardwood chips or chunks following the directions on page 43.

Sear the breasts over direct heat: bone-in, skin-on breasts for 7 to 10 minutes, boneless, skinless breasts for 5 to 6 minutes, turning a few times, until grill-marked and browned. Move to a cooler or unheated part of the grill and continue cooking, covered, until done: bone-in breasts for another 10 to 15 minutes, boneless breasts for 5 to 10 minutes more. Take the breasts off the grill at 155°F and let rest for 5 to 10 minutes. Chicken is done when the juices run clear and no pink is showing at the center.

Make the Basil-Garlic Oil: Puree all the ingredients in a blender or food processor.

Toss the green beans lightly in the Basil-Garlic Oil, reserving the excess oil, and grill them over direct heat on a perforated grid or in a grill basket, turning often, for 5 to 6 minutes until tender yet still crunchy. Do not overcook.

Arrange the green beans on a platter with the cherry tomatoes and basil leaves on top. Sprinkle with salt and pepper. Arrange the chicken breasts around the beans and spoon the remaining Basil-Garlic Oil over the vegetables and chicken. Serve with a chilled Pinot Grigio from northern Italy or Oregon.

Classic Grilled Chicken with Barbecue Sauce

Cooking chicken on the grill is an art, but one that can be easily mastered if you remember a few basics: Keep heat levels medium to high, move the chicken around on the grill to keep it from burning and to ensure that it is cooked through, and, above all, don't slather on barbecue sauce until the last few minutes of cooking. This sauce is made in the Kansas City style, tangy and sweet with just a bit of heat. Other regions prefer more or less sugar or molasses, vinegar or cayenne, and some use mustard rather than tomato as a base (see Mustard Barbecue Sauce, page 130). You could also use a store-bought sauce in this recipe, and heat it up, if you wish, with some cayenne or Tabasco.

Make the Barbecue Sauce: Stir the ingredients together in a saucepan and simmer over low heat for 20 to 30 minutes, stirring often, until thick and smooth. Divide the sauce into 2 portions, one for use in basting the chicken and one for serving at the table. (For safety's sake, discard any unused basting sauce).

Make the Herb and Pepper Rub: In a small bowl, mix all the ingredients together. Sprinkle the rub over all sides of the chicken pieces and refrigerate for up to 12 hours or let sit at room temperature for up to 1 hour. Bring the chicken to room temperature before grilling.

Prepare the grill for combination grilling-roasting at medium-high heat (350°F). Brush or spray the grill with oil. Add hickory, oak, or other hardwood chips or chunks following the directions on page 43.

Sear the chicken pieces over direct heat for 7 to 10 minutes, turning often. Move to a cooler or unheated part of the grill, cover, and continue cooking for 10 to 30 minutes, until the internal temperature reaches 155°F for breasts, and 160°F for thighs and legs or until the juices run clear and no pink shows at the center. Move cooked pieces to an unheated portion of the grill and brush them with barbecue sauce as the other pieces finish cooking. Brush all pieces with sauce about 5 minutes before removing them from the grill. Serve with reserved barbecue sauce and cold beer.

Barbecue Sauce

- 3 cups ketchup
- 1 cup tomato juice or beef stock
- ¼ cup molasses
- ¼ cup cider vinegar
- ¼ cup Worcestershire sauce
- 4 cloves garlic, minced
- 1 tablespoon hot Hungarian or Spanish paprika
- 1 tablespoon ancho chile powder or blended chili powder, preferably Gebhardt
- 1 tablespoon black pepper
- 1 teaspoon cayenne, or more to taste
- Salt and Tabasco or other hot sauce to taste

Herb and Pepper Rub

- ¼ cup sweet Hungarian or Spanish paprika
- ½ tablespoon hot Hungarian or Spanish paprika
- 2 tablespoons garlic powder
- 2 tablespoons dried sage
- 2 tablespoons dried oregano
- 1 tablespoon ancho chile powder or blended chili powder, preferably Gebhardt
- ½ tablespoon salt
- 1 teaspoon black pepper

- 1 (3-to 5-pound) chicken quartered or cut into 8 serving pieces; or 4 chicken breasts, bone-in, skin-on, or boneless, skinless; or 12 chicken thighs, bone-in, skin-on, or boneless, skinless

Spicy Chicken Thighs with Grilled Onions on Bacon-Wilted Greens

SERVES 4 TO 6

Spicy Rub

¼ cup sweet Hungarian or Spanish paprika

2 tablespoons chipotle powder or blended chili powder, preferably Gebhardt

1 tablespoon black pepper

2 tablespoons dry mustard

2 tablespoons brown sugar

2 tablespoons garlic powder

2 tablespoons onion powder

1 tablespoon dried thyme

1 tablespoon dried sage

½ tablespoon salt

12 chicken thighs, skin-on, bone-in, or skinless, boneless

2 large onions, cut into ½-inch rounds

Bacon-Wilted Greens

2 thick slices bacon

8 cups chopped cleaned greens (chard, kale, collards, mustard greens, turnip greens, or a mixture)

4 cloves garlic, chopped

2 tablespoons red-wine vinegar or cider vinegar

Chicken thighs are my favorite part of the bird to grill. They have just enough fat to take high heat and stay juicy on the grill, and I love their earthy flavor, especially when combined with a spicy rub or marinade. Just about every time I fire up the grill, I toss some onions or tomatoes over direct heat to brown and take on flavor from the smoke. I then use them with the dish, as the onions here, and save leftovers for sauces and salsas as in the Grilled Corn and Tomato Salsa recipe (page 94). The spicy rub is also good on pork.

Make the Spicy Rub: In a small bowl, mix all the ingredients together.

Sprinkle the chicken thighs generously with the spice rub on both sides. Put them in a resealable plastic bag or in a bowl with a lid, and let sit overnight in the refrigerator or up to 1 hour at room temperature. Bring them to room temperature before grilling.

Prepare the grill for combination grilling-roasting at medium-high heat (350°F). Brush or spray the grill with oil. Add oak, hickory, or other hardwood chips or chunks following the directions on page 43.

Brush or spray the chicken thighs and onion slices with oil. Sear the thighs on the highest heat for 2 to 3 minutes per side, moving to a cooler spot if flare-ups occur. Move the thighs to a cooler or unheated area, cover the grill, and cook until done: 5 to 7 minutes more per side for bone-in thighs, 3 to 5 minutes more for boneless. Chicken thighs are done when the internal temperature reaches 160°F or until the juices run clear and the meat shows no pink at the center. While the thighs cook on the cooler area, place the onion rounds on the hottest part of the grill and cook for 2 to 3 minutes per side, until they are grill-marked and beginning to soften. Remove from the grill as they are done.

GRILLED ONIONS

I prefer sweet onions (such as Maui, Vidalia, and Walla Walla) on the grill, but any large onion will do fine. I don't peel the onions (the papery skin usually burns off, but it helps to hold onion slices together); I just cut the onions into ½-inch or ¾-inch rounds. Brush or spray the slices with oil and place over medium-high heat. Grill on one side for 2 to 3 minutes, until nicely marked, and turn carefully with a spatula. Cook for another 2 to 3 minutes and remove. If the onion slices fall apart, don't worry. Just scrape them up any way you can and serve them; they'll still be delicious. I often grill onions and tomatoes while I am cooking other foods on the grill.

Cook the Bacon-Wilted Greens: Chop the bacon into coarse dice and cook in a large saucepan or skillet over medium heat until the fat is rendered out. When the bacon pieces are crisp, add all the greens and stir well. Stir in the garlic and vinegar and cover the pan. The greens will wilt and steam in the bacon fat, vinegar, and any water adhering to the greens from washing. If they begin to stick, add 1 to 2 tablespoons of water to the pan. Stir and cook the greens for 4 to 7 minutes, depending the type and age of the greens. Chard will cook quickly; kale, turnip, and mustard will take a little longer; tougher collards will take the most time.

Mound the greens and bacon on a platter and arrange the chicken and onions over the top. Amber ale is my drink of choice with this hearty dish, but a full-bodied California Zinfandel would also be delicious.

Hawaiian Chicken with Grilled Pineapple and Papaya Salad

SERVES 4

Hawaiian grill cooks work wonders with Asian style marinades for chicken, port, or fish, which they then grill over Kiawe wood. Kiawe wood sounds exotic, but it is simply mesquite that was originally brought to the islands by panaiolos, the cowboys that tend cattle herds on the Big Island. Grilling pineapple brings out the fruit's natural sweetness and adds a subtle, caramelized flavor that is irresistible, especially when paired with ginger and mint in this tangy salsa. Pork tenderloins make a tasty substitute for chicken in this dish; adjust the cooking times accordingly, following any of the pork tenderloin recipes in this book (pages 112, 114, and 117).

Make the marinade: In a bowl, mix all the marinade ingredients together. Pour the marinade over the chicken in a bowl with a lid or resealable plastic bag. Refrigerate overnight or let sit at room temperature for up to 1 hour, turning occasionally. Bring the chicken to room temperature, remove it from the marinade, and pat dry before grilling.

Prepare the grill for combination grilling-roasting over medium-high heat (350°F). Add mesquite or other hardwood chips or chunks following the directions on page 43.

Sear the chicken pieces over direct heat, moving to a cooler area if flare-ups occur, 3 to 4 minutes per side. Move to a cooler or unheated part of the grill, cover, and cook for 5 to 10 minutes more per side, until the internal temperature reaches 155°F for breasts and 160°F for thighs, or until the juices run clear and no pink shows at the center.

Meanwhile, make the salad: Grill the pineapple and onion slices over high heat for 2 to 3 minutes per side, until grill-marked and slightly browned. Remove from the grill and chop coarsely. In a large bowl, mix the pineapple and onion with the papaya, bell pepper, mint, and ginger. In a small bowl, whisk together the vinegar, orange juice, oils, and tamari. Pour the dressing over the salad and mix well. Taste for salt and chile oil.

Serve the chicken with the salad and Tedeschi dry pineapple wine from Maui or a dry Riesling from California or Alsace.

Hawaiian Marinade

- ¼ cup peanut or other vegetable oil
- 2 tablespoons sesame oil
- ¼ cup brown sugar
- ¼ cup tamari or soy sauce
- ¼ cup sweet sherry or sake
- ¼ cup chopped Maui or other sweet onions
- 4 cloves garlic, finely chopped
- 2 tablespoons finely chopped or grated ginger
- 2 teaspoons or more hot chile oil or other Asian hot sauce
- ¼ cup sesame seeds

- 12 chicken thighs, bone-in, skin-on, or boneless, skinless; or 4 chicken breasts, bone-in, skin-on, or boneless, skinless

Grilled Pineapple and Papaya Salad

- 1 fresh pineapple, peeled and cored, cut into ½-inch rounds
- 1 Maui or other sweet onion, cut into ½-inch rounds
- 2 cups coarsely chopped papaya
- 1 red bell pepper, seeded and finely chopped
- ½ cup chopped mint
- 2 tablespoons finely chopped or grated ginger
- 2 tablespoon rice vinegar
- Juice of 1 orange
- 3 tablespoons peanut or vegetable oil
- 1 tablespoon sesame oil
- 2 tablespoons tamari, or soy sauce
- Chile oil or other Asian hot sauce to taste
- Salt to taste

Smoked Chicken with Smoke-Roasted Pepper Coulis

SERVES 4 TO 6

Thyme and Garlic Paste

½ cup chopped fresh thyme or
   2 tablespoons dried

4 cloves garlic, minced

1 teaspoon salt

½ teaspoon black pepper

Olive oil

1 (4-to 5-pound) chicken

Smoke-Roasted Pepper Coulis

2 red bell peppers

1 clove garlic

Salt and pepper to taste

Olive oil

If you have a water smoker (see page 47) or offset smoker-cooker (see page 46), you'll get more smoke flavor by cooking this chicken at low temperatures (250°F to 300°F) using the long, slow cooking technique (see page 37). If you don't have one of these specialized smoker-cookers, you can get good results and good smoke flavor by cooking the chicken at higher temperatures (300°F to 325°F) for a shorter time in plenty of wood smoke in a covered grill. My advice is to cook smoked chicken any way you can and make a double recipe. I hardly ever cook just one smoked chicken: It's so delicious in salads, risotto, in sandwiches, and on pasta that I'm always happy to have some in the fridge.

Make the Thyme and Garlic Paste: In a blender, food processor, or mortar, mash together the thyme, garlic, salt, and pepper. Add enough oil to make a paste. Smear the paste all over the chicken, and under the skin wherever possible. Refrigerate the chicken, wrapped, for up to 12 hours or let sit at room temperature for up to 1 hour. Bring the chicken to room temperature before cooking.

Prepare a water smoker or offset smoker-cooker following the manufacturer's directions and pages 47 and 46. Or prepare a covered grill for indirect cooking at medium-low heat (300°F to 325°F). Brush or spray the grill with oil. Add hickory, oak, or other hardwood chips or chunks following the directions on page 43.

Place the chicken in the water smoker, offset smoker-cooker, or on the unheated portion of the covered grill, and smoke roast until done. The lower the ambient temperature of the smoker or grill, the longer the chicken will take. Figure on at least 2 to 3 hours at lower temperatures (250°F to 300°F), or 1 to 2 hours at higher temperatures (300°F to 325°F). It is important to check for doneness every 30 minutes or so using an instant-read meat thermometer. Chicken is done when the temperature reaches 160°F inside of the thigh, the juices run clear, and there is no pink showing near the bone. Let the chicken rest for 5 to 10 minutes.

BRUSCHETTA

These simple but delicious appetizers are easy to make and are a great way to keep hungry guests happy while you are grilling the main course. Slice baguettes or other French or Italian bread into ½-inch or ¾-inch rounds. Brush with herb- or garlic-flavored oil (see Flavored Oils, page 162) or with olive oil and a bit of garlic. Grill the bread over medium-high heat until marked and toasted. Remove and spread with a tangy topping. Some suggestions: coarsely pureed tomatoes hot off the grill with some fresh basil and garlic blended in; chopped grilled green chiles with lemon and grilled onions; a tapenade of roasted garlic and chopped, pitted black olives or Smoke Roasted Pepper Coulis.

Make the coulis: Roast the peppers in the smoker or on the unheated portion of the grill until soft, 30 minutes to 1 hour, depending on the temperature. Remove from the grill when they are beginning to collapse and let them cool in a sealed plastic or paper bag. Scrape off the skin and discard seeds and stems. In a food processor or blender, process the peppers together with the garlic, salt and pepper, and enough olive oil to make a puree.

Carve the chicken and serve it with the Smoke-Roasted Pepper Coulis and Smoked Tomato Risotto (page 96). A Côtes du Rhône or California Rhône-style red wine would be a good accompaniment.

Chile-Crusted Chicken Breasts with Grilled Corn and Tomato Salsa

SERVES 4

Chile Rub

¼ cup ancho chile powder, or blended chili powder, preferably Gebhardt

2 tablespoons garlic powder

2 tablespoons dried cilantro

1 tablespoon dried oregano

1 teaspoon ground cumin

½ tablespoon salt

4 chicken breasts, bone-in, skin-on, or boneless, skinless

Grilled Corn and Tomato Salsa

2 dried chiles such as ancho or pasilla (see page 60)

2 cups chopped grilled tomatoes (see page 103) or choped fresh or canned tomatoes

1 cup chopped grilled onions (see page 89)

1 cup cilantro leaves

2 cloves garlic

2 tablespoons Chile Rub or blended chili powder, preferably Gebhardt

Juice of 1 lemon

1 cup grilled corn kernels (see page 191) or cooked fresh or frozen corn kernels

Salt and hot sauce to taste

Chile and chicken breasts are a tasty combination: The spice of the chiles adds character to the somewhat bland meat, and the crust holds in the juices. I always cook double recipes of this dish, as I love to use the leftover chicken and salsa in tacos, burritos, and enchiladas (see Tacos, page 176). The salsa is wonderful with grilled fish or pork and will last, covered in the refrigerator, for a week or so. The Chile Rub will keep in a covered jar for a few months. For choosing, handling, and preparing dried chiles, see Chiles, page 60.

To make the Chile Rub: Mix the ingredients together in a small bowl.

Sprinkle the rub generously on all sides of the chicken breasts and refrigerated, tightly wrapped, for up to 12 hours or let sit at room temperature for up to 1 hour. Bring the chicken to room temperature before grilling.

Prepare the grill for combination grilling-roasting at medium-high heat (350°F). Brush or spray the grill with oil. Add mesquite or other hardwood chips or chunks following the directions on page 43.

Sear the breasts over direct heat: bone-in, skin-on breasts for 7 to 10 minutes, boneless, skinless breasts for 5 to 6 minutes, turning a few times, until grill-marked and browned. Move to a cooler or unheated part of the grill and continue cooking, covered, until done: bone-in breasts for another 10 to 15 minutes, boneless breasts for 5 to 10 minutes more. Take the chicken breasts off the grill at 155°F and let rest for 5 to 10 minutes. Chicken is done when the juices run clear and no pink is showing at the center.

Make the Grilled Corn and Tomato Salsa: Soak the dried chiles in hot water to cover for about 30 minutes. Break open and remove and discard the seeds and stems. Tear up the chiles and put them in a blender or food processor. Add the tomatoes, onions, cilantro, garlic, Chile Rub, and lemon juice. Process briefly to form a coarse puree. Pour the puree into a bowl and stir in the corn. Taste for salt and heat levels.

Serve chicken breasts with the salsa, Campfire Beans (page 150), and Grilled Tortillas (page 116), along with cold Mexican beer.

Chicken Cacciatore with Fusilli and Grilled Pepper-Tomato Sauce

SERVES 4

Pasta of any kind makes a great base for grilled foods, especially when combined with a smoky sauce based on grilled tomatoes, peppers, and mushrooms. I use chicken here, but use your imagination and follow your tastes. Swordfish, large prawns, pork tenderloin, or skewered beef could be easily substituted in this recipe, with delicious results. Many recipes in this book provide leftovers that are very tasty served over pasta (see Pasta, page 97).

Make the marinade: In a bowl, mix all the ingredients together. Pour the marinade over the chicken pieces in a bowl with a lid or in a resealable plastic bag, and refrigerate for up to 12 hours or let sit at room temperature for up to 2 hours, turning occasionally. Bring the chicken to room temperature, remove from the marinade, and pat dry before grilling.

Prepare the grill for combination grilling-roasting at medium-high heat (350°F). Add hardwood chips or chunks following the directions on page 43.

Sear the chicken over direct heat until browned and grill-marked, for 7 to 10 minutes, turning often. Move the chicken to a cooler or unheated part of the grill and cook, covered, for another 10 minutes to 30 minutes, or until done: 155°F for breasts, 160°F for thighs and legs. Breasts will be done sooner than thighs and legs or quarters. There should be no pink at the center or near the bone, and the juices should run clear.

Meanwhile, make the Grilled Pepper-Tomato Sauce: Coat or spray the tomatoes, peppers, mushrooms, and the onion slices with oil. Use a grill basket or perforated grid if it looks like the vegetables might fall through the grill. Grill the tomatoes, peppers, mushrooms, and onion slices over direct heat, turning often, until grill-marked and beginning to soften. Remove the vegetables as they cook: tomatoes will need only a few minutes, onions, mushrooms, and peppers should cook for 4 to 10 minutes total. Remove the stems and seeds from the peppers and scrape away most of the skin. Chop the vegetables coarsely and mix with the chopped garlic, herbs, and salt and pepper. Stir in a few dashes of oil if you wish.

Cook the fusilli in boiling salted water. Drain and mix with half the sauce. Arrange the chicken pieces on top and spoon on the remaining sauce. Serve with Chianti Classico from Tuscany.

Italian Marinade

1 cup olive oil

¼ cup balsamic vinegar

6 cloves garlic, finely chopped

1 onion, chopped

¼ cup chopped fresh basil or 2 tablespoons dried

¼ cup chopped fresh oregano or 2 tablespoons dried

½ tablespoon salt

1 teaspoon black pepper

1 teaspoon red pepper flakes

4 chicken breasts, boneless, skin-on or skinless; or 8 chicken thighs, boneless, skin-on or skinless; or 1 whole chicken, quartered

Grilled Pepper-Tomato Sauce

4 medium tomatoes

1 red bell pepper

1 yellow bell pepper

8 large mushrooms

1 large onion, cut into ½-inch rounds

Olive oil

4 cloves garlic, chopped

¼ cup chopped fresh basil or 2 tablespoons dried

2 tablespoons chopped fresh oregano or 1 tablespoon dried

Salt and pepper to taste

1 pound fusilli or other dried pasta

Roast Chicken with Tarragon and Smoked Tomato Risotto

SERVES 4 TO 6

Lemon-Tarragon Paste

½ cup chopped fresh tarragon
   or ¼ cup dried

Juice and grated zest of 1 lemon

3 cloves garlic

1 teaspoon salt

1 teaspoon lemon pepper

Olive oil

1 (5-pound) roasting chicken

1 lemon, quartered

1 onion, quartered

Sprigs of fresh tarragon or ¼ cup dried

Smoked Tomato Risotto

2 cups chopped grilled tomatoes
   (see page 103) or chopped fresh or
   canned tomatoes

1 cup or more chicken stock

½ cup or more white or rosé wine

2 tablespoons butter

½ cup finely chopped onions

1 cup Arborio or other Italian rice

2 tablespoons chopped fresh tarragon or
   1 tablespoon dried

1 cup fresh or frozen peas

¼ cup grated Parmesan

Salt and pepper to taste

Roasting a whole chicken on a covered grill is the best way I know of to get a crisp, browned skin and succulent, juicy meat. Add to this the flavors of lemon, garlic, tarragon, and wood smoke, and you have the centerpiece of a dramatic and delicious meal. If you have a rotisserie attachment, this is a good time to use it. You could also cook the chicken over indirect heat over a drip pan or use an upright roasting rack or the beer can method, putting the lemon, onion, and tarragon sprigs inside the can (see Beer Can Chicken, page 98). The lemon tarragon paste is also good on fish.

Make the Lemon-Tarragon Paste: In a blender, food processor, or mortar, mash the tarragon, lemon juice, lemon zest, garlic, salt, and lemon pepper together. Add enough oil to make a paste. Rub all over the chicken and under the skin wherever possible. Put the lemon quarters, onion, and tarragon sprigs in the cavity. Tie the legs and wings to the body.

Prepare the grill for rotisserie cooking or indirect cooking at medium-high heat (350°F). Brush or spray the grill with oil. Add alder, apple, or other hardwood chips or chunks following the directions on page 43.

Arrange the chicken on a spit, following the rotisserie manufacturer's directions and page 48, or place the chicken on an unheated portion of the grill over a drip pan. Roast, covered, for 1 to 1½ hours, until the temperature inside the thigh reaches 160°F, the juices run clear, and no pink shows near the bone. Remove from the grill and let rest for 5 to 10 minutes.

Meanwhile, make the risotto: In a blender or food processor, process the tomatoes in 1 cup stock and ½ cup wine. Pour into a saucepan, bring to a boil, and then lower the heat to keep warm. In another saucepan, melt the butter, add the onions, and lightly sauté for 5 to 6 minutes over medium heat. Add the rice and stir to coat it with the butter and onions; cook for 3 to 5 minutes, stirring constantly. Add 1 cup of the tomato-wine mixture, along with the tarragon, and cook over medium heat, uncovered, stirring occasionally, until all the liquid is absorbed. Stir in another 1 cup of the liquid and cook, stirring, until it is absorbed. Continue to add liquid and stir

PASTAS

Well, I'm not ready to provide a recipe for spaghettini alla griglia or barbecued ravioli—not yet anyway—but I really think that pasta is at its best when topped with, say, pieces of smoky, garlicky chicken, and a sauce of chopped grilled tomatoes, onions, and peppers mixed together with fresh garlic and basil from the garden. You can't grill the pasta, but you can grill just about everything else that goes on the plate.

I provide a number of tomato sauces made from grilled tomatoes (see pages 182–83), and any of these, of course, would be tasty over pasta. But think of finding in the fridge a couple of cups of leftover Garlic Shrimp on the Grill with Lime Aïoli (page 68). Why not mix chopped shrimp and aïoli with a cup or two of leftover grilled eggplant and one or two chopped grilled tomatoes, and spoon this savory combination over fusilli or linguine? Virtually any recipe in this book could be chopped and tossed with your favorite pasta, from Grilled Lobster with Garlic and Tarragon Butter (page 80) to Peppery Duck Breast with Creole Gravy (page 102), Smoke-Roasted Tri-Tip with Orange and Chile Glaze (page 147) to Grilled Summer Squash with Fresh Herb Marinade (page 179). Just get the pasta water boiling, take some delicious grilled food out of the reefer, and put together a delicious pasta dinner for family or friends.

until the rice is just barely tender, 20 to 30 minutes. Add more wine or stock, as necessary. A few minutes before the rice is done, stir in the peas, along with a little more liquid. When the rice is tender, stir in the cheese and taste for salt and pepper.

Carve the chicken and serve it with the risotto and a light-bodied Pinot Noir from California's south coast or from Oregon.

Bacon-Wrapped Quail or Game Hens, Campfire Style

SERVES 4

8 quail or 4 Cornish game hens

1 orange cut into eighths or quarters

1 onion, cut into eighths or quarters

1 rib celery, cut into chunks

16 fresh sage leaves or 2 tablespoons dried sage

8 thick slices bacon

Coarsely ground black pepper

Game birds like quail, squab, or pheasant are quite lean and often need to be wrapped with bacon or thin slices of pork back fat for them to be tender and juicy. The recipe below calls for 8 quail or 4 game hens to serve 4 diners, but you could easily substitute 2 pheasants or 4 large squab. Sage is especially delicious with poultry. Try to find fresh sage for this recipe, although dried sage will do. Sage is such a colorful and delicious herb—why not plant it in your garden or in a pot on a sunny kitchen window ledge?

Prepare the grill for indirect cooking over medium-high heat (350°F) with a drip pan under the unheated part of the grill. Brush or spray the grill with oil. Add hardwood chips or chunks following the directions on page 43.

Stuff the birds with pieces of orange, onion, and celery. Divide up the sage leaves and arrange them on the breasts and thighs of the birds or sprinkle with dried sage. Wrap the birds with the bacon, and tie with butcher's string across the breasts and around the thighs and legs. Sprinkle the birds with pepper.

Sear the birds over direct heat, turning carefully, for 5 to 7 minutes, until they are lightly browned. Move to the unheated part of the grill over the drip pan and continue cooking until done. Quail will cook more quickly than larger game hens: Check the internal temperatures after 30 minutes. Poultry is done when the inner part of the thigh registers 160°F, the juices run clear, and no pink is showing near the bone. Remove the birds from the heat and let rest for 5 to 10 minutes.

Cut and discard the strings and serve the birds whole with Grilled Summer Squash with Fresh Herb Marinade (page 179). A Côtes du Rhône from southern France makes a fine accompaniment.

Peppery Duck Breast with Creole Gravy

SERVES 4

Peppery Spice Rub

2 tablespoons sweet Hungarian or Spanish paprika

1 tablespoon black pepper

1 tablespoon white pepper

1 tablespoon onion powder

½ teaspoon cayenne

½ teaspoon ground coriander

½ teaspoon ground dried ginger

1 teaspoon salt

4 boneless duck breasts

Creole Gravy

2 tablespoons rendered duck fat or vegetable oil

2 tablespoons flour

1 jalapeño chile, seeded, and finely chopped

¼ cup finely chopped red bell pepper

¼ cup chopped green onions

¼ cup finely chopped celery

1 tablespoon Peppery Spice Rub

1 teaspoon dried thyme

1 cup chopped grilled tomatoes (see page 103) or chopped fresh or canned tomatoes

1½ cups duck or chicken stock

2 tablespoons Worcestershire sauce

2 tablespoons molasses

2 tablespoons tomato paste

1 ounce bourbon or other whiskey (optional)

Salt and Tabasco or other hot sauce to taste

Duck breast is one of the tastiest things you can put on the grill. It has a high fat content, so it stays juicy after grilling, and its dark, succulent meat takes well to savory herbs and spices. Use boned breasts (what the French call magrets) from Peking, muscovy, or wild duck for this recipe. Each type of duck has its own size and flavors, but all are delicious. The trick to cooking duck on the grill is to render out the fat without causing a conflagration. Keep the fire on the medium to low side and watch out for flare-ups. Move the duck to a cooler part of the grill if the fire flares up or let it roast on the unheated portion if the fire seems to be getting out of hand. Adjust cooking times and temperatures as you need to. The main thing is to get the internal temperature to about 135°F, or medium-rare, the fat rendered out, and the skin crisp. This spice rub is also good on chicken.

Make the spice rub: In a small bowl, mix all the ingredients together.

Remove any visible fat from the duck breasts and score the skin once or twice with a sharp knife then prick all over with the tip of the knife. Reserving 1 tablespoon of the spice mixture, rub both sides of the breasts generously with the spice mixture. Refrigerate the duck, tightly wrapped, for up to 12 hours or let sit at room temperature for up to 1 hour. Bring the duck to room temperature before cooking.

Prepare the grill for direct cooking over medium-low heat (300°F to 325°F). Add hardwood chips or chunks following the directions on page 43.

Grill the duck breasts, skin side down, over direct heat for 7 to 12 minutes, moving to a cooler spot on the grill if flare-ups occur. The skin should be crisp and brown and the fat rendered. Turn and cook for another 5 to 6 minutes or more, to the medium or medium-rare stage, about 135°F, pink at the center, and quite juicy. Let the duck rest, loosely covered in foil, for 5 to 10 minutes.

Make the Creole Gravy: In a heavy skillet or saucepan over medium heat, stir the rendered duck fat together with the flour to make a roux. Cook and

GRILLED TOMATOES

Grilling whole tomatoes for a few minutes adds immeasurably to their flavor and softens them slightly for use in sauces. The technique couldn't be simpler: Brush or spray whole tomatoes with oil and place them directly over medium-high heat on the smokiest part of the grill. Turn them often, scorching and marking them on all sides; remove when they are beginning to soften and the skin is breaking. This should only take a few minutes, depending on the size of the tomato. I often grill tomatoes on one part of the grill while I cook steaks or chops over direct heat, or poultry or larger meat cuts by indirect heat. I take the tomatoes off the fire and puree them coarsely in the blender to use in a sauce or salsa. If you have a large amount of tomatoes in late summer, grill them in batches and freeze them whole in resealable plastic bags for use over the winter months.

stir for a few minutes until the roux becomes tan or a light peanut butter color. Stir in the chile, bell peppers, green onions, celery, spice rub, and thyme and continue to cook, stirring constantly, for 2 to 3 minutes, until the vegetables start to soften. Stir in the tomatoes and stock, along with the Worcestershire sauce, molasses, tomato paste, and optional bourbon. Continue cooking and stirring over medium-low heat for 10 to 12 minutes, until the gravy is thick and smooth. Taste for salt and heat levels and adjust accordingly.

Spoon the gravy over the duck breasts and serve with Grilled Herb Polenta (page 145) or Grilled Garlic Grits (page 114) and Hot Greens (page 123). California Syrah or Australian Shiraz would balance the spice and richness of this dish.

Roast Duck with Ginger-Honey Glaze

Roasting a whole duck on the grill ensures a crisp exterior and tender, juicy meat. Duck has a good amount of fat under the skin, so be sure to prick the skin all over before roasting so that the fat can drip away as the duck cooks. A rotisserie is ideal here: The fat bastes the meat as it cooks and ends up in the drip pan underneath. Indirect cooking with a drip pan under the duck will also work well.

Spice Rub
2 tablespoons ground dried ginger

1 tablespoon onion powder

1 teaspoon ground coriander

1 teaspoon white pepper

1 teaspoon lemon pepper

1½ teaspoons salt

1 (4-to 5-pound) duck

1 lemon, quartered

1 onion, quartered

Ginger-Honey Glaze
¼ cup honey

¼ cup sweet sherry

2 tablespoons grated or finely chopped fresh ginger

Juice of 1 lemon

Prepare the grill for indirect cooking over medium-low heat (300°F to 325°F). Add hardwood chips or chunks following the directions on page 43.

Make the spice rub: In a small bowl, mix all the ingredients together.

Remove any visible fat from the duck and prick the skin all over with the tip of a sharp knife. Rub the skin of the duck and inside the cavity generously with the spice mixture and put the lemon and onion inside the bird. Place a large drip pan under the area of the grill the duck will be cooking on.

Arrange the bird on a spit over the drip pan, following the manufacturer's directions and page 48, or place the duck on the unheated portion of the grill for indirect cooking. Cover the grill and cook for 1 hour. Remove the duck from the grill and carefully take out the drip pan. Discard the fat from the pan along with any fat that has accumulated in the body cavity. Replace the pan and put the duck back on the grill. Check the pan and the duck cavity from time to time to see if excess fat is accumulating. If it is, discard the fat, as above.

Cook the duck for about 1 more hour, until the internal temperature inside the leg reaches 160°F and the skin is brown and crisp. Start checking after about 1½ hours' total cooking time. There should be no pink showing near the bone and the juices should run clear. If the skin looks like it is browning too fast, cover lightly with aluminum foil and reduce the heat by lowering the dials with a gas grill or closing the vents and not adding new coals on a charcoal grill.

Make the Ginger-Honey Glaze: Mix the ingredients together in a small bowl. About 15 minutes before the duck is finished, brush generously with the Ginger-Honey Glaze. Baste a few more times before removing from the grill and brush again with the glaze just before serving.

Chipotle Turkey or Chicken Thighs

SERVES 4

4 turkey thighs or 8 chicken thighs,
   bone-in, skin-on, or boneless, skinless

1 (7-ounce) can chipotles en adobo

Chipotle Salsa

2 or more chipotles en adobo

2 cups chopped grilled tomatoes
   (see page 103) or chopped fresh
   or canned tomatoes

1 cup chopped grilled onions
   (see page 89)

1 cup cilantro leaves

2 cloves garlic

Juice of ½ lemon

Salt to taste

Turkey or chicken thighs are perfect for grilling because of their higher fat content and flavorful meat. One turkey thigh makes a hearty serving for one diner, and leftovers are great for tacos or burritos or over pasta. Chipotles en adobo are dried, smoked ripe jalapeño chiles canned in a spicy tomato sauce (see Ingredients, page 54). They are widely available in Latino and specialty markets and can be ordered by mail (see Sources, page 200).

If you wish, remove the thigh bone from each turkey thigh with a thin sharp knife. Remove the skin or leave on as you wish. Reserve 2 or more chipotles for the salsa. In a food processor or blender, briefly process the chipotles en adobo to a coarse paste. Rub all over the turkey or chicken thighs, and under the skin if left on. Let the thighs sit for up to 2 hours at room temperature before grilling.

Prepare the grill for combination grilling-roasting at medium-high heat (350°F). Brush or spray the grill with oil. Add mesquite or other hardwood chips or chunks following the directions on page 43.

Sear the thighs over direct heat, turning often, until lightly browned and grill-marked. Turkey thighs should take about 10 minutes; bone-in, skin-on chicken thighs, 6 to 7 minutes; boneless, skinless chicken thighs, 4 to 5 minutes. Move thighs to the unheated portion of the grill, cover, and cook until done, when the internal temperature registers 160°F, juices run clear, and no pink is showing. Turkey thighs should take about 15 minutes more; bone-in chicken thighs another 8 to 10 minutes; and boneless thighs, 5 to 8 minutes more.

Make the Chipotle Salsa: In a food processor or blender, process the chipotles, tomatoes, onions, cilantro, garlic, and lemon juice to a coarse puree. Taste for salt.

Serve the thighs with the salsa and Campfire Beans (page 150) along with Dos Equis or another amber lager.

Roast Turkey with Herb and Pepper Rub and Smoke-Roasted Yams

Roasting turkey in a covered grill is easy and turns out a flavorful, and smoky version of this holiday favorite. But don't wait for the holidays to cook this dish. A summer night is a good time to roast outdoors, and all that good smoke should keep the mosquitoes away. Leftover turkey makes wonderful sandwiches and salads, and even tacos, burritos, or enchiladas when paired with a tangy salsa (such as Grilled Corn and Tomato Salsa, page 94). A small turkey (8-to 12-pounds) works best on the grill, especially if you are using a rotisserie. Huge birds strain the spit motor and are often too large for kettle grills to cook properly. The Herb and Pepper Rub is also good on chicken and pork.

Herb and Pepper Rub

- ¼ cup chopped fresh thyme or 2 tablespoons dried
- ¼ cup chopped fresh sage or 2 tablespoons dried
- 4 cloves garlic, minced
- 2 tablespoons grated lemon zest
- 1 tablespoon lemon pepper
- 1 teaspoon black pepper
- ½ tablespoon salt

- 1 (8-to 12-pound) turkey
- 1 lemon, quartered
- 1 rib of celery
- 1 onion, quartered

Smoke-Roasted Yams

- 6 to 8 yams
- ¼ pound salted butter, softened
- ¼ cup molasses
- Juice of ½ lemon
- Salt and pepper

Prepare the grill for indirect cooking or rotisserie cooking over medium-high heat (350°F), with a drip pan under the unheated portion of the grill. Add hardwood chips or chunks, following the directions on page 43.

Make the Herb and Pepper Rub: In a small bowl, mix all the ingredients together.

Pull off and discard any fat from the turkey and tie the wings and legs against the body. Rub the skin of the turkey with the cut lemon and sprinkle all over, including in the cavity, with the herb mixture. Place the lemon, celery, and onion in the cavity. Place the turkey over the drip pan on the unheated part of the grill or arrange it on the rotisserie, following the manufacturer's directions and page 48. Roast, covered, until done: Turkey is done when the temperature of the inner thigh reaches 160°F, the juices run clear, and no pink is showing near the bone. Start checking the turkey after 1 hour with an instant-read meat thermometer or by making a small cut inside the thigh with the tip of a sharp knife. If the turkey seems to be browning too quickly, cover loosely with foil. Let the turkey rest for 10 to 15 minutes, loosely tented with foil.

Make the Smoke-Roasted Yams: Scrub the yams and prick with a fork or tip of a knife. Place on an unheated part of the grill or a roasting rack and bake until a knife goes in easily, about 1 hour. Mix together the butter, molasses, and lemon juice and spoon the mixture into the opened yams when serving. Sprinkle the yams with salt and pepper.

Carve the turkey and serve with the yams.

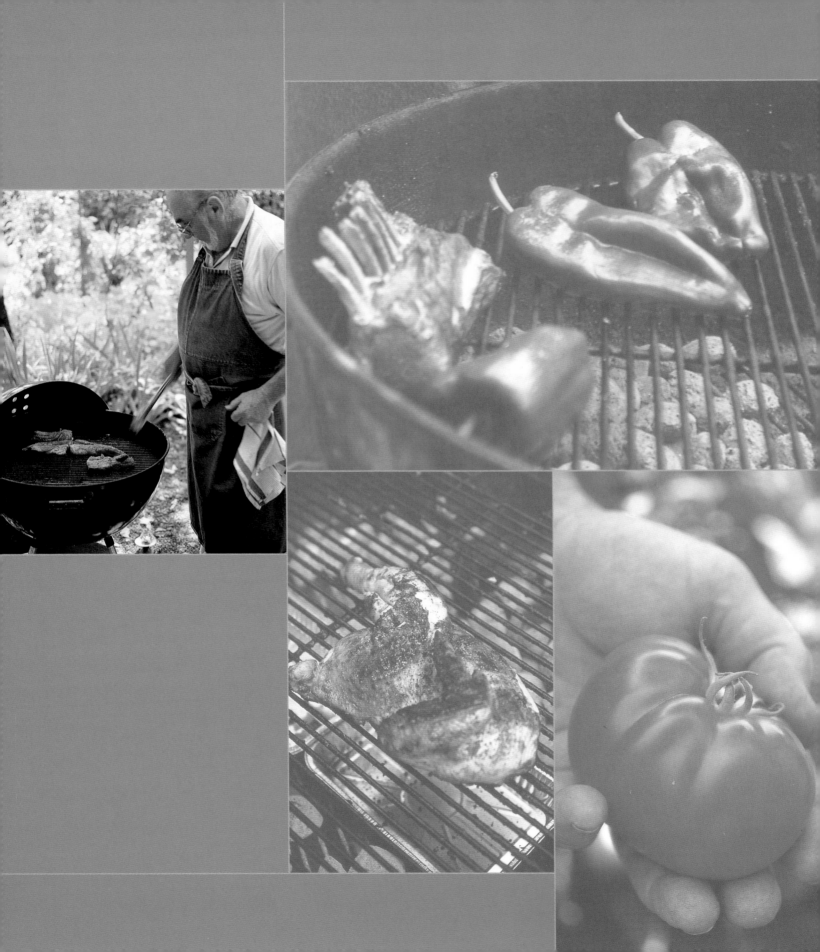

Pork is the most versatile meat and is delicious when cooked correctly on the grill. Today's leaner pork is more healthful than the fat porkers our grandmothers cooked, but you have to be careful not to overcook it. All too often pork is cooked until it is so dry and tough that it is virtually inedible. The parasite trichinia is killed at 138°F or medium-rare, and lean pork loin and tenderloin need not be cooked higher than 150°F for safety; many professional chefs remove pork loin chops and tenderloins from the grill at 145°F and let them rest while the internal temperature rises a few more degrees. A meat thermometer is an essential tool for cooking lean pork; you can also cut into the center: A bit of pink with a creamy white color will ensure juicy and tender pork.

The cut of pork will determine the type of cooking required and how long to cook it. Pork tenderloin, the pig's equivalent of beef fillet, is a very tender, lean strip of meat that runs along the backbone. Tenderloin is one of my favorite meats for the grill. One tenderloin will serve two people, either whole as a small roast, cut into two serving pieces and butterflied, or cut into small collops or boneless chops. Larger pieces of tenderloin should be cooked by combination grilling-roasting, while smaller and thinner pieces can be grilled directly over medium-high heat. Tenderloin's mild, sweet flavor takes well to sauces, glazes, and marinades. Be wary of marinades that contain citrus or other acidic liquids; if pork tenderloins are left in an acidic marinade too long, they can become mushy. Marinate them no more than a few hours before grilling.

Pork chops are the most popular cut of pork. They can be cooked successfully on the grill, but be very careful not to cook chops too long. Thinner chops (less than ½ inch) are tricky to grill. A few minutes on either side on direct medium-high heat is usually all that is needed to cook them to about 150°F, slightly pink in the center. Pork chops are delicious when seasoned with a spicy, chile-based rub. Leftovers provide opportunities for great tacos and burritos for lunch or dinner. Pork loin or rib chops should be cooked to 150°F to remain juicy and tender; fattier and chewier shoulder chops or pork steaks are better cooked to 160°F, with no pink showing at the center.

Pork loin roasts are a great favorite at my house, and I often spit-roast bone-in or boneless pork loin with delicious results. Roasts can also be cooked over indirect heat. I especially like to smear the roast with a savory paste of garlic and fresh herbs before roasting. Wood smoke is a welcome addition to pork's succulent meat; I prefer hickory, but oak and mesquite are also tasty. Use a meat thermometer with pork loin and remove the roast from the fire at or just below 150°F and let the roast sit for 10 minutes before carving.

Pork ribs are especially good on the grill. The type of ribs determines the mode of cooking: Baby back ribs from the loin are tender and cook relatively quickly by combination grilling-roasting; country-style ribs, cut from the shoulder, need to cook longer by combination grilling-roasting or indirect cooking over medium heat; tougher spareribs from the belly require long slow cooking on low indirect heat to become tender. Sweet barbecue sauce should be brushed on only during the last few minutes of cooking, although mops based on vinegar, beer, chiles, and other non-sweet liquids are often used as basting sauces throughout cooking.

Pork shoulder and fresh ham are both wonderful cuts for slow-roasting in a kettle grill, water smoker, or offset smoker-cooker. Slow-roasting over medium-low to low heat dissolves collagen or connective tissue and renders out the fat to provide luscious and tender meat. Shoulder and ham should be cooked to at least 160°F, although barbecue pit cookers reach much higher internal temperatures.

Pork Tenderloin with Chipotle Rub and Grilled Chiles and Onions

SERVES 4

Chipotle Rub

2 tablespoons chipotle chile powder or blended chili powder preferably Gebhardt

2 tablespoons sweet Hungarian or Spanish paprika

1 tablespoon garlic powder

1 tablespoon onion powder

1 tablespoon dried oregano

1 tablespoon dried cilantro

1 teaspoon ground cumin

½ tablespoon salt

2 (1½-pound) pork tenderloins

4 Anaheim or other large green chiles (see Chiles, page 60)

2 sweet onions (Maui, Vidalia, Walla Walla), cut into ½-inch slices

2 limes

Salt and pepper

½ cup chopped fresh cilantro

Pork tenderloin's sweet, tender meat melds wonderfully with herbs, spices, and chiles. Here we rub the meat with chipotle powder and spices and grill the tenderloins along with green chiles and sweet onions. Chipotles, dried, smoked red jalapeño chiles, come in a variety of forms: dried chiles, canned in adobo sauce, or ground into powder (see Chiles, page 60). Chipotle powder is widely available in markets today (McCormick, for example, makes an excellent version) or it can be ordered by mail (see Sources, page 200). If you can't find it, you can substitute a blended chili powder, but you'll lose the uniquely smoky and fiery flavors of the chipotle.

Make the Chipotle Rub: In a small bowl, mix all the ingredients together.

Trim any fat and silverskin from the tenderloins. You may cut them across the grain into round boneless chops about ¾-inch thick; or butterfly them by cutting lengthwise down the center, leaving about ½ inch of meat, and then pounding flat; or leave them whole. If you butterfly or leave the tenderloins whole, cut each tenderloin in half crosswise to make 4 individual servings. Sprinkle all sides generously with the rub and refrigerate, tightly wrapped, for up to 12 hours or let sit at room temperature for up to an hour. Bring the pork to room temperature before grilling.

Prepare the grill for combination grilling-roasting at medium-high heat (350°F). Brush or spray the grill with oil. Add mesquite or other hardwood chips or chunks, following the directions on page 43.

Sear the tenderloins over high heat for 3 to 4 minutes per side. This should be enough to cook the chops to doneness: Pork is done when the internal temperature reaches 150°F, and it is firm to the touch, and slightly pink at the center. Move larger pieces of pork to a cooler part of the grill, cover, and cook until done, about 5 more minutes for butterflied tenderloins, 7 or more for whole tenderloins. Do not overcook.

GRILLED PEPPERS

Fresh whole peppers are easy to grill, and the light char they receive from the fire adds immeasurably to their taste. You can easily grill them while you cook other foods. Brush or spray whole, unpeeled bell or large green chile peppers (see Chiles, page 60) with oil and place over high heat. Grill for 5 to 7 minutes or longer, depending on the size and shape of the pepper, until the skin is scorched and charred all over. Remove the pepper from the grill and put into a sealed plastic or paper bag for 10 to 15 minutes. Remove the pepper from the bag, scrape off the skin, and remove the stem and seeds. Chop or slice the pepper as you wish and use it in a salsa or serve as directed in the recipe.

Grill the chiles over high heat, turning often, until charred and softened, 7 to 10 minutes. Remove from the heat and place in a sealed plastic or paper bag for about 15 minutes. Scrape the skin off and remove and discard stems and seeds. Chop the chiles coarsely and place them on a platter. Grill the onions for 3 to 5 minutes, turning once or twice, until grill-marked and starting to soften. Chop coarsely and strew the onions over the chiles.

Squeeze 1 lime over the chiles and onions and cut the other into eighths for garnish. Sprinkle the chiles and onions with salt and pepper, top with the pork tenderloin chops or pieces. Garnish with the limes and sprinkle with cilantro. Serve with an amber ale or a light red wine such as Beaujolais.

Pork Tenderloin with Sage and Black Pepper Rub and Garlic-Chile Grits

SERVES 4

Garlic-Chile Grits

2 cloves garlic, minced

¼ cup chopped mild green chiles, such as Anaheim (see Chiles, page 60)

1 teaspoon salt

½ teaspoon black pepper

1 tablespoons butter or vegetable oil

1 cups quick-cooking grits, preferably Albers

Sage and Black Pepper Rub

¼ cup dried sage

2 tablespoons garlic powder or granulated garlic

2 tablespoons onion powder

2 tablespoons brown sugar

½ tablespoon salt

1 tablespoon black pepper

2 (1½-pound) pork tenderloins

Pork tenderloin is a versatile cut for grilling. The tenderloin is the fillet of the pig, a tender and virtually fatless strip of succulent meat that lies along the backbone. It can be cut into small, boneless chops, butterflied, or left whole, as you prefer. One tenderloin will serve two diners amply, and if you have any leftovers the meat is delicious on sandwiches, cut into strips for composed salads, or mixed with tomato sauce over pasta. Because it is so low in fat, care must be taken when cooking tenderloin. Do not overcook it: Remove tenderloin from the grill when the internal temperature of the thickest part reaches 150°F or when it is still quite juicy and slightly pink at the center. Grits, a Southern staple, can be flavored, cooked, and cooled and, just like polenta, cut into squares and grilled. The sage and black pepper rub is also good on chicken.

Prepare the grits the day before or at least 2 hours before you want to grill the pork: Combine the garlic, chiles, salt, pepper, butter, and 4 cups water in a large saucepan, bring to a boil, and stir in the grits. Reduce heat to low, cover, and cook, stirring occassionally, for about 15 minutes or until the grits are thick and soft. Pour the grits onto a greased baking pan to a thickness of about 1 inch. Let cool and refrigerate for at least 2 hours.

Make the Sage and Black Pepper Rub: In a small bowl, mix all the ingredients together.

Trim any fat and silverskin from the tenderloins. You may cut them across the grain into round boneless chops about ¾ inch thick, or butterfly them by cutting lengthwise down the center, leaving about ½ inch of meat, and then pounding them flat; or leave them whole. If you butterfly or leave the tenderloins whole, cut each tenderloin in half crosswise to make 4 individual servings. Sprinkle all sides generously with the sage and pepper rub and refrigerate, tightly wrapped, for up to 12 hours or let sit at room temperature for up to an hour. Bring the pork to room temperature before grilling.

Prepare the grill for combination grilling-roasting at medium-high heat (350°F). Brush or spray the grill with oil. Add hardwood chips or chunks following the directions on page 43.

GRILLED TORTILLAS

You can make your own tortillas from commercial masa dough or flour (follow the directions on the package) or buy corn or wheat tortillas. Many Hispanic markets will sell you prepared dough or the masa flour; and you can often buy excellent handmade tortillas from Mexican markets and restaurants. Grilling tortillas is simple: If you are using fresh dough, place the newly made tortilla over medium-high heat for 2 to 3 minutes per side, until toasted and nicely marked; turn and cook for another 2 to 3 minutes until done. Precooked store-bought corn or wheat tortillas simply need to be grill-marked and warmed through for 1 to 2 minutes per side. Precooked tortillas can also be scorched and heated through by placing them directly on a gas burner on a stove for 1 to 2 minutes per side.

Sear the tenderloins over high heat for 3 to 4 minutes per side. This should be enough to cook the chops to doneness: Pork is done when the internal temperature reaches 150°F, it is firm to the touch, and slightly pink at the center. Move larger pieces of pork to a cooler part of the grill, cover, and cook until done, about 5 more minutes for butterflied tenderloins, 7 or more for whole tenderloins. Do not overcook. Grill the grits: Cut into 4-inch squares. Brush or spray both sides with oil and grill directly over high heat for 3 or more minutes per side, until grill-marked and lightly browned.

Serve the tenderloins with the grilled grits, Roasted Red-Pepper Coulis (page 92), and Grilled Portobello Mushrooms with Garlic and Basil Oil (page 190). A full-bodied rosé from southern France's Tavel or Bandol regions would accompany this dish nicely.

Pork Tenderloin Marinated in Rum and Ginger with Grilled Pineapple–Onion Relish

SERVES 4

Asian cooks love pork since the meat seems to absorb flavors better than any other. And in Hawaii, grill chefs often marinate pork in soy, pineapple and citrus juices, and ginger to create a unique, island flavor—once you've tasted it, you never forget it. Be careful, however, with marinades like this one that include acidic liquids like fruit juice and sugar. Don't marinate delicate pork tenderloins too long or they can become mushy, and be careful not to char the meat on too hot a fire.

Rum and Ginger Marinade

1 cup soy sauce

½ cup finely chopped Maui or other sweet onion

¼ cup dark rum

¼ cup pineapple or orange juice

½ teaspoon vanilla extract

2 tablespoons brown sugar

2 tablespoons finely chopped ginger

2 tablespoons finely chopped garlic

Juice of 2 limes

½ teaspoon or more Asian hot chile oil

2 (1½-pound) pork tenderloins

Grilled Pineapple–Onion Relish

8 (½-inch thick) slices fresh pineapple

1 Maui or other sweet onion, cut into ½-inch rounds

2 tablespoons chopped ginger

2 tablespoons tamari or soy sauce

½ teaspoon vanilla extract

Juice of 1 lime

2 tablespoons rice vinegar

1 tablespoon sesame oil

2 tablespoons peanut or other vegetable oil

Salt and Asian hot chile oil to taste

Make the marinade: In a bowl, mix all the ingredients together.

Trim any fat and silverskin from the tenderloins. You may cut them across the grain into round boneless chops about ¾ inch thick; or butterfly them by cutting lengthwise down the center leaving about ½ inch of meat and then pounding flat; or leave them whole. If you butterfly or leave the tenderloins whole, cut each tenderloin in half crosswise to make 4 individual servings. Pour the marinade over the pork and marinate at room temperature for no more than 2 hours.

Prepare the grill for combination grilling-roasting at medium-high heat (350°F). Brush or spray the grill with oil. Add mesquite or other hardwood chips or chunks following the directions on page 43.

Sear the tenderloins over high heat for 3 to 4 minutes per side. This should be enough to cook chops to doneness: Pork is done when the internal temperature reaches 150°F, and it is firm to the touch and slightly pink at the center. Move larger pieces of pork to a cooler part of the grill, cover, and cook until done, about 5 more minutes for butterflied tenderloins, 7 or more for whole tenderloins. Be careful of charring (because of the sugar in the marinade) and do not overcook.

Make the relish: Grill the pineapple and onion slices for 3 to 4 minutes per side, until grill-marked and heated through. Remove from the grill, chop coarsely, and put into a large bowl. In a small bowl, combine the ginger, tamari, vanilla, lime juice, vinegar, sesame oil, and peanut oil. Pour over the onions and pineapple and mix well. Taste for salt and add a dash or two of Asian chile oil, if you like.

Serve the pork with the relish, along with Eggplant Grilled in Oregano Smoke (page 178) and a fragrant, dry Riesling from Germany or Alsace.

Cajun Pork Chops with Dirty Rice

SERVES 4

Cajun Spice Rub

¼ cup sweet Hungarian or
   Spanish paprika

1 tablespoon hot Hungarian or Spanish
   paprika, or more to taste

1 teaspoon cayenne, or more to taste

¼ cup garlic powder or granulated garlic

2 tablespoons onion powder

1 tablespoon ground dried bay leaves
   or filé powder

½ tablespoon salt

1 tablespoon black pepper

Dirty Rice

2 tablespoons vegetable oil

2 chicken or duck livers, chopped

½ cup chopped green onions or scallions,
   white and green parts

1 red bell pepper, finely chopped

1 tablespoon Cajun Spice Rub

1½ cups long-grain rice

3 cups chicken stock, tomato juice,
   or water

Tabasco or other hot sauce to taste

Salt and pepper to taste

4 pork loin or rib chops,
   at least 1 inch thick

Folks in Cajun country, around New Orleans, love pork and they love spices. You can hot up this rub with more cayenne or hot paprika, according to your taste. Ground bay leaf is sometimes hard to find. You can order it by mail (see Sources, page 200), grind up bay leaves yourself in a spice grinder, or use filé powder, a Creole mix of ground thyme and sassafras often used in gumbo. Dirty rice is a favorite Cajun accompaniment to pork, seafood, or sausages. It too can be spiced up to taste by the addition of another Creole staple, Tabasco, made in Louisiana from fermented chiles. If you use canned chicken stock, be careful with the salt.

Make the Cajun Spice Rub: In a small bow, mix together the ingredients.

Make the Dirty Rice: Heat the oil in a large pot over medium-high heat and stir in the livers, green onions, bell pepper, and spice rub. Cook for 3 to 4 minutes, stirring often. Stir in the rice until it is well coated and then add the stock and Tabasco. Bring to a boil, then cover and cook over low heat for 20 minutes, or until the rice is tender and the liquid is absorbed. Add more liquid during cooking if needed. Taste for salt, pepper, and more Tabasco.

Prepare the grill for direct cooking over medium-high heat (350°F). Brush or spray the grill with oil. Add hardwood chips or chunks following the directions on page 43.

Trim any excess fat from the chops and slash the edges to prevent curling. Rub the chops all over with the spice rub. Sear over medium-high heat for 4 to 5 minutes per side, turning once or twice. Move to a cooler area of the grill if flare-ups occur. Check for doneness with a meat thermometer (pork loin is done when the internal temperature reaches 150°F) or cut into a chop to see if the meat is firm and slightly pink near the bone. If the chops need more cooking, move them to a cooler or unheated part of the grill, cover, and cook until done. Let the chops rest, lightly tented with foil, for 5 minutes.

Serve the pork chops on top of the dirty rice with Grilled Corn with Chile-Garlic Butter (page 179) and Dixie beer or another light lager.

Chinatown Country-Style Ribs with Hoisin-Mustard Glaze

SERVES 4 TO 6

Chinese Marinade

1 cup soy sauce

¼ cup chopped onions

4 cloves garlic, minced

¼ cup sweet sherry or sake

2 tablespoons hoisin sauce

2 tablespoons chopped fresh ginger

2 teaspoons five-spice powder

1 teaspoon Asian chile oil, or more to taste

4 pounds country-style pork ribs

Hoisin-Mustard Glaze

½ cup hoisin sauce

¼ cup sweet sherry or sake

Juice of 1 lime

1 clove garlic, minced

1 tablespoon dry mustard

Country-style pork ribs are long, butterflied chops cut from the pork shoulder and can be found bone-in and boneless. They need to cook a bit longer than baby back ribs from the loin and are tender much sooner than spareribs, which come from the belly section of the pig and require long, slow cooking (see Ribs, Ribs, Ribs, page 127). Country-style ribs, like most pork, take well to Chinese and other Asian seasonings. This marinade includes hoisin sauce, a sweet and pungent Chinese sauce based on soy, and Chinese five-spice powder, a blend of ground star anise, Szechuan pepper, fennel, cloves, and cinnamon (see Ingredients, page 54). Both are available in most markets or by mail order (see Sources, page 200).

Make the marinade: In a bowl, stir the ingredients together thoroughly. Pour the marinade over the ribs in a bowl with a lid or a resealable plastic bag and refrigerate for up to 12 hours or marinate at room temperature for up to 2 hours. Bring the ribs to room temperature, remove from the marinade, and pat dry before grilling.

Make the glaze: In a bowl, mix all the ingredients together.

Prepare the grill for indirect grilling over medium-low heat (300°F to 325°F). Add hardwood chips or chunks following the directions on page 43.

Place the ribs on the unheated portion of the grill over a drip pan and roast, covered, for 1½ to 2 hours, or until done. The internal temperature should register 165°F, and the meat should be very tender and pulling away from the bones. During the last 30 minutes of cooking, brush 3 or 4 times with the Hoisin-Mustard Glaze.

Serve the ribs with Sweet and Sour Rice (page 69) and a dark Munich lager.

Smoke-Roasted Country Ribs with Vinegar-Chile Mop and Hot Greens

SERVES 4 TO 6

Pork and woodsmoke are a natural pairing, and country-style ribs have enough fat to take the longer cooking required to really get some smoke flavor into the meat. Basting slow-cooked pork or beef with a savory and pungent mop or basting liquid is a tradition in the South and Southwest. You not only keep the meat moist and juicy, but you add more flavor and spice the longer it cooks. I like to add whatever mop I'm using to greens or beans or a sauce that accompanies the meat to pick up the flavors and round out the dish.

4 pounds country-style ribs

Chile Rub (see page 94 or 153) or other spice rub

Vinegar-Chile Mop

2 dried ancho or pasilla chiles (see Chiles, page 60)

2 cups chopped grilled tomatoes (see page 103) or chopped fresh or canned tomatoes

3 cloves garlic

1 (12-ounce) bottle dark ale

¼ cup white vinegar

¼ cup molasses

Tabasco or other hot sauce to taste

Salt to taste

Hot Greens

8 cups washed chopped greens (chard, kale, collards, turnip greens, mustard greens, or a mixture)

1 cup sliced onions

4 cloves garlic, crushed

¼ cup Vinegar-Chile Mop

Juice of ½ lemon

1 teaspoon Tabasco or other hot sauce, or more to taste

Salt and pepper to taste

Coat the ribs thoroughly with the spice rub and refrigerate for up to 12 hours or let sit at room temperature up to 2 hours. Bring the ribs to room temperature before grilling.

Make the Chile-Vinegar Mop: Soak the dried chiles in hot water to cover for at least 30 minutes. Drain them, then remove and discard the seeds and stems. Place the chiles in a food processor or blender and add the tomatoes and garlic. Process to make a coarse puree. In a bowl combine the puree with the remaining ingredients. Reserve ¼ cup of the mop for the greens.

Prepare the grill for indirect cooking over medium-low heat (300°F to 325°F). Add hickory, oak, or other hardwood chips or chunks following the directions on page 43.

Place the ribs on the unheated portion of the grill over a drip pan and roast, covered, for 1½ to 2 hours, or until done, turning occasionally. The internal temperature should register 165°F, and the meat should be very tender and pulling away from the bones. Begin basting with the mop after 30 minutes of cooking and baste often until done.

Make the Hot Greens: Put the greens, onions, garlic, the reserved ¼ cup of the mop, the lemon juice, and Tabasco in a large covered Dutch oven or skillet over medium-high heat and stir well. The greens will wilt and steam. If they begin to stick, add 1 to 2 tablespoons of water to the pan. Stir and cook the greens for 4 to 7 minutes, depending the type and age of the greens. Chard will cook quickly; kale and turnip and mustard greens will take a little longer, tougher collards will take the most time. Taste for salt, pepper, and hot sauce. They should be spicy.

Serve the ribs with the Hot Greens, Smoke-Roasted New Potatoes (page 149), and a dark ale or a Syrah from southern France.

Chile-Ginger Baby Back Ribs with Plum Sauce Glaze

SERVES 4

Chile-Ginger Marinade

1 cup peanut or other vegetable oil

½ cup tamari or soy sauce

¼ cup mirin or sweet sherry

¼ cup chopped ginger

¼ cup chopped green onions

4 cloves garlic, chopped

Juice of 2 limes

2 jalapeño or serrano chiles, seeded, and finely chopped (see Chiles, page 60)

2 racks baby back ribs

Plum Sauce Glaze

1 cup Chinese plum sauce

¼ cup mirin or sweet sherry

2 tablespoons chopped ginger

1 tablespoon minced garlic

Dash of Asian chile oil, or more to taste

Baby back ribs marinated in chiles, ginger, and garlic are delicious when brushed with a savory, sweet glaze made from Chinese plum sauce, garlic, and ginger. This marinade and glaze would also work well with country-style ribs (pages 122, 123), pork chops (page 120), and pork tenderloin (pages 112, 114, 117). Be careful with pork tenderloin, however, and don't marinate it for more than a couple of hours in any acidic marinade such as this one. Chinese plum sauce and Asian chile oil (see Ingredients, page 54) are available in most markets and Asian groceries and by mail order (see Sources, page 200).

Make the marinade: In a large bowl, mix all the ingredients together. Pour over the ribs in a bowl with lid or in resealable plastic bags, and refrigerate for up to 12 hours, turning occasionally, or marinate at room temperature for up to 2 hours. Bring the ribs to room temperature, remove from the marinade and pat dry before grilling.

Prepare the grill for indirect cooking over low heat (300°F to 325°F), with a drip pan under the unheated portion of the grill. Add mesquite or other hardwood chips or chunks, if you wish, following the directions on page 43.

Make the glaze: In a small bowl, mix all the ingredients together.

Sear both sides of both racks over direct heat for 3 to 4 minutes per side. Move the ribs to the middle of the grill over the drip pan and cook, covered, for 2 to 2½ hours, turning occasionally. Add more hardwood chips or chunks as needed for smoke. Test the ribs for tenderness after about 1½ hours. When done, the internal temperature should register at least 165°F, and the meat should be very tender and juicy, although not falling off the bones. During the last 30 minutes of cooking, baste the ribs often with the Plum Sauce Glaze. After removing them from the grill, baste the ribs generously with the glaze, wrap them in heavy-duty foil, and let rest for 10 to 15 minutes.

Cut the ribs between the bones and serve with any remaining Plum Sauce Glaze and Sweet and Sour Rice (page 69).

Peppery Baby Back Ribs with Smoky Tomato Barbecue Sauce

SERVES 4

Baby back ribs are trimmed from the pork loin and yield tender, succulent meat without a great amount of cooking (see Ribs, Ribs, Ribs, page 127). Give them as much hickory or oak smoke as you can and roast them at moderately low temperatures in a covered grill for about 2 hours in the fragrant wood smoke. Baste with barbecue sauce only for the last 30 minutes of cooking. The rub below is a creation of Jeff Clark, my nephew and an accomplished grill cook and barbecue pit man. He developed and tested many of the classic 'cue recipes in this book.

Make Jeff's Rib Rub I: In a small bowl, mix all the ingredients together.

Coat the ribs generously with the rub, wrap them in heavy-duty foil, and refrigerate overnight or let sit at room temperature for up to 1 hour. Bring the ribs to room temperature before grilling.

Make the Smoky Barbecue Sauce: Stir the ingredients together in a saucepan and bring to a simmer; cook for 20 to 30 minutes, stirring often, until thick and smooth. Taste for heat levels and salt.

Prepare the grill for indirect cooking over medium-low heat (300°F to 325°F), with drip pan under the unheated portion of the grill. Add plenty of hickory, oak, or other hardwood chips or chunks following the directions on page 43.

Unwrap the ribs and sear both sides of both racks over direct heat for 3 to 4 minutes per side. Move the ribs to the middle of the grill over the drip pan and cook, covered, for 2 to 2½ hours, turning occasionally. Add more hardwood chips or chunks as needed for smoke. Test the ribs for tenderness after about 1½ hours. When done, the internal temperature should register at least 165°F, and the meat should be very tender and juicy, although not falling off the bones. During the last 30 minutes of cooking baste the ribs often with the Smoky Tomato Barbecue Sauce or your favorite barbecue sauce. After removing the ribs from the grill, baste them generously with the sauce, wrap them in heavy-duty foil, and let rest for 10 to 15 minutes.

Slice the ribs between the bones and serve with any remaining barbecue sauce, Campfire Beans (page 150), and plenty of napkins.

Jeff's Rib Rub I

3 tablespoons dry mustard

1 tablespoon Hungarian or Spanish sweet paprika

1 tablespoon ground cumin

1 tablespoon dried oregano

1 tablespoon dried cilantro

2 tablespoons brown sugar

1 teaspoon black pepper

½ tablespoon salt

2 racks baby back ribs

Smoky Tomato Barbecue Sauce

2 cups chopped grilled tomatoes (see page 103) or chopped fresh or canned tomatoes

1 cup chili sauce or ketchup

¼ cup molasses

¼ cup prepared yellow mustard

2 tablespoons Worcestershire sauce

2 tablespoons vinegar

Juice of 1 lemon

4 cloves garlic, minced

1 teaspoon cayenne, or more to taste

Tabasco or other hot sauce to taste

Salt to taste

Slow-Cooked Spareribs, Two Ways

SERVES 2 TO 4 AS A MAIN COURSE

Jeff's Rib Rub II

1 tablespoon ground annato seeds (achiote, see ingredients page 54) or paprika

1 tablespoon ancho chile powder or blended chili powder, preferably Gebhardt

2 teaspoons dry mustard

2 teaspoons ground cumin

2 teaspoons dried thyme

2 tablespoons brown sugar

2 teaspoons garlic powder

½ teaspoon cayenne

1 teaspoon salt

1 (3- to 4-pound) rack of pork spareribs

Barbecue sauce, homemade (pages 87, 125, or 130) or store-bought (optional)

Spareribs are cut from the belly of the pig and require long, slow cooking in wood smoke to be at their tender, succulent best. Mention spareribs to any barbecuer worth his salty rub, and you are sure to get an argument about how to season and cook spareribs: whether to use a rub or a mop or a sauce or all or none of the above; to wrap in foil and precook or parboil or prebake or not; to sear or not to sear; to cook in hickory or oak or pecan smoke; or to use some arcane mix of seasonings, methods, and woods that the 'cue expert you're arguing with has come up with. It's really a matter of preference, after all. But one thing is sure: You do need to get the ribs tender, and that requires some version of long and slow cooking, no matter how you do it. I've given a couple of techniques here that turn out delicious ribs. There are many other ways to cook a tasty rib, however, and I'm looking forward to trying them all.

Make Jeff's Rib Rub II: In a small bowl, mix all the ingredients together.

Coat the ribs generously with the spice rub, wrap them in heavy-duty foil and refrigerate for up to 12 hours or let sit at room temperature for up to 2 hours. Bring the ribs to room temperature before cooking.

Method I: Long, Slow Cooking

Prepare a kettle grill, water smoker, or offset smoker-cooker (see pages 45–47) for indirect cooking over very low heat (225°F to 250°F). While still wrapped in foil, bake the ribs on the unheated portion of the grill or smoker for 1 hour. Unwrap the ribs and cook them over direct heat for 4 to 5 minutes per side. Add hardwood chips or chunks following the directions on page 43. Smoke-roast the ribs, meaty side up, on the unheated portion of the grill for another 2 hours or more. If you like, brush the ribs with barbecue sauce during the last 30 minutes of cooking. When the meat is very tender and the rib bones are starting to become exposed at the edges, take the ribs off the grill. Brush again with barbecue sauce, if you wish, and wrap them in heavy-duty foil. Let the ribs rest for at least 15 minutes. Slice the ribs between the bones and serve with barbecue sauce at the table, if desired.

RIBS, RIBS, RIBS

Pork ribs are barbecue favorites, but you should know what type of ribs you are cooking before you put them on the grill. Classic barbecued ribs are most likely to be spareribs cut from the belly of the hog. Spareribs have little meat, plenty of bone, and a goodly amount of fat. They are best cooked long and slow to get the meat in between the ribs tender enough to eat and to render out the fat. When properly cooked for many hours on a low-temperature, smoky fire, they become luscious and delicious. (See Slow-Cooked Spareribs, Two Ways, page 126).

Baby back ribs are a modern invention, a result of selling cuts of pork boned and packaged in Cryovac. These ribs are the bones of the loin that are removed to make boned loin roast or boned loin chops. They can be quite meaty, if cut correctly, but are sometimes mostly bone. Look for plenty of meat on the bones with just a thin layer of fat. Baby back ribs are relatively tender and can be cooked successfully on a medium fire for a shorter time that true

spareribs. They are delicious when marinated and/or glazed with a spicy sauce and smoke-roasted in a kettle grill (see Chile and Ginger Baby Back Ribs with Plum Sauce Glaze, page 124, and Peppery Baby Back Ribs with Smoky Tomato Barbecue Sauce, page 125).

Country-style ribs are cut from the pork shoulder and can be found boneless or bone-in. They are best cooked at medium temperature for an hour or two to become tender and to render out fat. They are very meaty and a better value than either of the other pork rib cuts and are a favorite cut of Chinese cooks (see Chinatown Country-Style Ribs with Hoisin Mustard Glaze, page 122, and Smoke-Roasted Country Ribs with Vinegar-Chile Mop and Hot Greens, page 123).

Beef ribs, trimmed from the prime rib to make boneless rib-eye roasts and steaks, are popular and tasty; they can be seasoned with a spice rub and grilled directly over medium-high heat to the medium or medium-rare stage.

Method II: Indirect Cooking

Prepare a kettle grill for indirect cooking over medium-low heat (300°F to 325°F). Add hardwood chips or chunks following the directions on page 43. Unwrap the ribs, sear them over direct heat for 4 to 5 minutes per side, then move them to the unheated portion of the grill. Smoke-roast the ribs, meaty side up, for another 2½ to 3 hours. If you like, brush the ribs with barbecue sauce during the last 30 minutes of cooking. When the meat is very tender and the rib bones are starting to become exposed at the edges, take the ribs off the grill. Brush again with barbecue sauce, if you wish, and wrap them in heavy-duty foil. Let the ribs rest for at least 15 minutes. Slice the ribs between the bones and serve with barbecue sauce at the table, if desired.

Carolina Pulled Pork
with Mustard Barbecue Sauce

Jeff's Pork Rub

¼ cup chile powder, or blended
   chili powder, preferably Gebhardt

2 tablespoons ground cumin

3 tablespoons dried oregano

3 tablespoons garlic powder

2 tablespoons onion powder

2 tablespoons brown sugar

1 tablespoon dry mustard

2 teaspoons black pepper

1 tablespoon salt

1 (10-pound) pork shoulder, skinned or
   1 (5-pound) pork shoulder butt or
   fresh picnic roast

Mustard Barbecue Sauce

2 cups prepared yellow mustard

1 cup ketchup

2 tablespoons Worcestershire sauce

¼ cup molasses

2 tablespoons white vinegar

Juice of 1 lemon

1 teaspoon or more cayenne

1 teaspoon black pepper

Tabasco or other hot sauce to taste

Another rub and recipe developed by pit master Jeff Clark, this is a version of the classic Carolina pulled pork, where pork shoulder, fresh ham, or even a whole porker, is slow-cooked over a smoky fire for hours until the meat falls (or can be pulled, hence the name) off the bones. There's some discussion about the right barbecue sauce to use on pulled pork among native Carolinians (now that I think of it, there's always some discussion about barbecue sauce). Some folks prefer a thin, tomato and vinegar–based sauce, others ladle on a mustard–based sauce, as here. Whatever way you like it, pulled pork is a luscious, savory treat that's worth the wait. We've given you the long, slow method (Method I), which requires an offset smoker-cooker (see page 46) and a quicker way (Method II) to enable you to cook pulled pork in a kettle barbecue. Both are delicious.

Make Jeff's Pork Rub: In a small bowl, mix the ingredients together.

Rub the spice mixture generously over the pork shoulder. Wrap in heavy-duty foil and refrigerate for up to 12 hours or let sit at room temperature for up to 2 hours. Bring the pork to room temperature before cooking.

Make the Mustard Barbecue Sauce: Whisk the ingredients together in a saucepan over low heat and simmer for 7 to 8 minutes. Let cool before using.

Method I: Long, Slow Smoking

In an offset smoker-cooker (see page 46), start a small amount of charcoal in the firebox. While the coals burn, take the roast out of the refrigerator and allow it to come to room temperature. When the coals are completely gray, spread them in a single layer and add soaked wood chunks (preferably hickory). Put the roast in the smoker, maintaining the heat at 200° to 250°F. Smoke-roast for 6 to 8 hours for a half-shoulder, 10 to 12 hours for a whole shoulder. Add hickory chunks periodically to maintain the correct temperature. At some point the fire will have no remaining charcoal and will be made up entirely of wood. This is ideal, but a mixture of dry and soaked wood chips will have to be added to maintain the correct temperature. When the roast reaches an internal temperature of 190°F, take it off the smoker, wrap it in heavy-duty

BARBECUE SAUCE

There is probably no subject more likely to get a good argument going than barbecue sauce. It seems that just about everybody has an opinion and there seems to be a decided lack of the compromising spirit among proponents of regional styles. The type of barbecue sauce that's found on most supermarket shelves is a version of the Kansas City style (in fact one of the better commercial sauces is called simply Kansas City Barbecue Sauce), a thick, tangy and decidedly sweet tomato-based sauce. Most of these sauces are mild and a bit sweet, the word bland often leaps to mind when tasting them, but they are usually pleasant enough, if used correctly.

The problem is not usually with the barbecue sauce, but how it is used. All too often backyard chefs pour sauce on the chicken or burgers as they go on the fire, and then keep brushing sauce on as the food chars in the flames. The sugar in the thickened sauce clings to the food and caramelizes in the hot fire that most backyard grillers like to build. Chicken and burgers both need to be cooked through for safety's sake, and too often these foods end up charred on the outside and raw inside, not a pleasant prospect. If you are going to use a commercial barbecue sauce, and I rarely do, brush it on the food only for the last few minutes of cooking or just serve it as a table sauce and let diners put it on the food themselves.

In recipes, use your favorite sauce or try one of our recipes (see Classic Grilled Chicken with Barbecue Sauce, page 87, or Peppery Baby Back Ribs with Smoky Tomato Barbecue Sauce, page 125).

foil, and let rest for 20 to 30 minutes. After letting the meat rest, it should shred easily with a fork. Pull the meat from the bone into bite-size pieces. Serve on your favorite sandwich or hamburger buns with the Mustard Barbecue Sauce, accompanied by Grilled Corn with Chile-Garlic Butter (page 191).

Method II: Indirect Grilling

Prepare a kettle grill for indirect cooking over low heat (250°F to 300°F), with a drip pan under the unheated portion of the grill. Take the pork roast from the refrigerator 1 hour before cooking. Place the roast, still wrapped in foil, over drip pan. Roast for 1½ hours for a half shoulder, 3 hours for a whole shoulder. Remove the roast, unwrap it, and put it back on the grill over the drip pan. Add hardwood chips or chunks following the directions on page 43. Roast for 1 additional hour, or more, until the surface is nicely browned and the meat is very tender and pulling away from the bone. The internal temperature should register 190°F. Remove the roast from the grill, wrap it in heavy-duty foil, and let it rest for 20 to 30 minutes. Pull the meat from the bone and serve on your favorite sandwich or hamburger buns with the Mustard Barbecue Sauce, accompanied by Grilled Corn with Chile-Garlic Butter (page 191).

Glazed Smoked Ham with Pineapple-Chile Chutney

Most American ham is already smoked and cooked, but just about every one I've ever tasted could benefit from some time roasting in oak or hickory smoke in a covered grill. Add a tangy glaze and some chutney on the side and you have a combination that brings out the rich, smoky flavor that ham lovers adore. Use a shank or butt half of a presmoked, precooked bone-in ham here, one simply labeled "ham" without any reference to added water. Do not use a deli ham or canned ham or something labeled "ham and water product." (See Ingredients, page 54.) If you can find a precooked high-quality smokehouse ham, all the better (see Sources, page 200). The glaze is also delicious on roast pork loin.

Rum, Mustard, and Molasses Glaze

- 1 cup Dijon mustard
- ¼ cup molasses
- 2 tablespoons dark rum
- 2 tablespoons pineapple juice, or more to taste
- 2 tablespoons ancho chile powder, or blended chili powder, preferably Gebhardt
- ½ half precooked smoked ham (7 to 9 pounds), preferably bone-in

Pineapple-Chile Chutney

- 1 pineapple, peeled, cored, and coarsely chopped
- 1 sweet onion (Maui, Vidalia, Walla Walla), coarsely chopped
- 1 red bell pepper, seeded and finely chopped
- 1 jalapeño chile, seeded, deveined, and finely chopped
- 1 cup raisins
- 1 lemon, peeled and thinly sliced
- 1 cup pineapple juice
- ¼ cup white vinegar
- ¼ cup brown sugar
- 1 teaspoon ground allspice
- 1 teaspoon ground cinnamon
- ¼ teaspoon ground cloves

Prepare the grill for indirect cooking over medium-high heat (350°F), with a drip pan under the unheated portion of the grill. Add hickory, oak, or other hardwood chips or chunks following the directions on page 43.

Make the glaze: In a small bowl, whisk all the ingredients together.

Place the ham over the drip pan on the unheated portion of the grill and roast, covered, for 1 hour. Remove from the heat and adjust the burners or add more coals to the fire to raise the temperature to high (375°F to 400°F), adding more hardwood chips or chunks for smoke. Remove any skin from the ham and cut away and discard excess fat. Score the remaining fat in a crisscross pattern and brush the ham with the glaze. Put the ham back on the grill and cook, covered, for 30 minutes or more, brushing often with the glaze. When the ham is nicely glazed and brown, remove it from the grill and let rest for 10 minutes before carving.

Make the Pineapple-Chile Chutney: In a nonreactive pan, combine all the ingredients and bring to a boil. Lower the heat to a simmer and cook for 10 to 12 minutes. Remove from the heat and let cool.

Serve the ham with the chutney and Smoke-Roasted Yams (page 107). A dry Alsatian or Austrian Riesling pairs well with smoked ham and the sweet-tart chutney.

Beef

Americans love the beefsteak. From the earliest days of our cooking, a thick steak "hot and sputtering from the griddle" has been the ideal centerpiece of American celebrations. Steak is the perfect meat for the backyard grill: succulent and tender, full of beefy flavor, easy to cook. Loin or top sirloin are best for direct grilling. Porterhouse, New York strip, and rib steak, to name a few, are all delicious when seasoned with a spice rub or herb and garlic paste and grilled over medium-high heat. Other, slightly chewier steaks, such as flank, skirt, chuck, or top round, can be marinated to add flavor and enhance tenderness.

I like to trim steaks of external fat, but I search out steaks with plenty of internal fat or marbling to ensure tenderness. If you can find USDA Prime or Choice steaks, use these on the grill; or look for deep red meat with plenty of

STEAKS

Steaks cut from the loin or back of the steer near the hip are among the tenderest cuts of beef and are best grilled over a medium-high fire; they are usually tender enough to go directly on the grill with just some salt and pepper or a spice rub. Other steaks from the sirloin, the flank and other areas are a bit chewier and can benefit from spending some time in a tangy marinade. Chuck steaks from the shoulder and top round steaks from the rump need a marinade to be tender enough to grill.

Steak nomenclature can be confusing, as cuts are given different names in different regions. Following are the most common cuts with variant names.

The tenderest steaks are the top loin steaks: fillet or beef tenderloin, also called tournedos, filet mignon, Châteaubriand, fillet steak; strip or loin steak, also called New York strip steak, Kansas City steak, club steak, Delmonico steak, shell steak; rib steak, also called rib-eye steak, Spencer steak, market steak. Steaks from the sirloin are called sirloin steak, top sirloin steak, butt steak, culotte steak, and triangle steak. (See Porterhouse Steak with Smoky Spice Rub, page 138, New York Strip Steak or Shell Steak with Thyme and Garlic Paste, page 140, Chile-Bourbon Sirloin Steak, page 139.)

Flank steak, also called London broil, skirt steak, also called fajita meat, and hanger steak, also called hanging tenderloin and butcher's steak, are tender cuts, but a little chewier than top loin or sirloin steaks. They often benefit from soaking in an acidic marinade (see Skirt Steak or Flank Steak with Citrus-Chile Marinade, page 142).

Some chuck steaks can be grilled successfully after time in a marinade: flatiron steak (quite tender), blade steak, mock tender steak, and chuck-eye steak. Top round steak, also called London broil, can be grilled after marinating. Other cuts from the chuck and round, such as Swiss steak and round steak, are too tough to grill and are better braised.

marbling. If you get flare-ups when grilling steaks, move them to a cooler area of the grill, and cover a kettle grill. I don't like the older practice of squirting water (or pouring beer) over flaming steaks; you just get more fat into the fire, wash off seasonings, and prevent a savory crust from forming on the surface of the meat.

Another favorite American meat on the grill is the burger. Although many have scorned the fast-food burgers that seem to be taking over the world, an authentic American hamburger, carefully cooked and seasoned, is absolutely delicious. The key is to purchase the right type of ground meat: Ground chuck containing about 20% fat is ideal. Fattier ground beef (up to 30% fat) makes a greasy burger that will shrink and flare up on the grill; leaner ground sirloin or round (about 15% fat) produces a dry and crumbly burger. Some stores these days sell ground beef labeled with the fat content or (oddly) the lean content; ground chuck, for example, might be labeled 80% lean ground beef. True burger lovers choose their own piece of chuck and have the butcher grind it for them. Be sure to tell him that you intend the meat for hamburgers to ensure good-quality meat.

There is a safety consideration with ground beef: You must cook hamburgers to at least the medium-well stage (160°F) to kill *E. coli* and any other harmful bacteria. I eat steak or roast beef rare because the surface of the meat is seared to well over 160°F and the compact interior has no place for bacteria to develop; grinding meat, on the other hand, breaks up the structure of the muscle and allows for bacterial growth throughout the meat. Sterilizing the surface won't help; you have to get the higher level of heat throughout the meat for safety's sake. So it's good-bye to rare burgers and definitely no more steak tartare for me.

Tender beef roasts such as beef fillet or prime rib can be excellent when spit-roasted or cooked by indirect heat in a kettle grill. A savory spice rub or herb paste adds plenty of flavor, and wood chips, especially oak or mesquite, add a smoky undertone.

Porterhouse Steak with Smoky Spice Rub

SERVES 4

Smoky Spice Rub

¼ cup sweet Spanish smoked paprika or other paprika

2 tablespoons chipotle chile powder or a blended chili powder, preferably Gebhardt

2 tablespoons garlic powder

1 tablespoon dried rosemary or thyme

½ tablespoon salt

½ tablespoon black pepper

2 porterhouse steaks, 2 inches thick

The porterhouse, which includes a generous portion of the beef fillet and a piece of the loin, is my favorite steak on the grill. Its full, beefy flavor takes well to spices, and one thick porterhouse divides perfectly into two serving portions, plus the juicy bone to argue about. The full effect of the Smoky Spice Rub depends on using Spanish smoked paprika made from smoked dried peppers (see Ingredients, page 54) and/or chipotle powder, ground dried and smoked jalapeños. Spanish smoked paprika is available from specialty stores and by mail order (see Sources, page 200) and is worth the effort to find. Chipotle powder is available from McCormick Spice Company, which sells to most major markets, and by mail order. If you can't find either, use regular paprika and blended chili powder with plenty of wood smoke. The rub is also delicious on pork or chicken.

Make the spice rub: In a small bowl, mix all the ingredients together.

Cut away most of the external fat from the steaks and slash the edges in 2 or 3 places to prevent curling. Sprinkle all sides of the steaks with the spice rub and wrap them in plastic wrap or put them into a resealable plastic bag. Refrigerate for up to 12 hours or let sit at room temperature for up to 1 hour. Bring the steaks to room temperature before cooking.

Prepare the grill for direct cooking over medium-high heat (350°F), making sure that you have three levels of heat on the grill: medium-high heat, medium heat, and low or no heat (see page 36). Brush or spray the grill with oil. Add hickory, oak, mesquite, or other hardwood chips or chunks following the directions on page 43.

Sear the steaks over medium-high heat for 5 to 6 minutes per side, turning once or twice, moving them to a cooler part of the grill if flare-ups occur. Move the steaks to a cooler or unheated area of the grill and cook, covered, until done. For rare steak the internal temperature should register 120°F to 125°F and the meat should be red near the bone; medium-rare should register 130°F to 135°F and be pink near the bone. Remove the steaks and let rest for 5 minutes. Carve each into two pieces: the fillet portion and the loin portion. Serve one piece to each diner and let the carnivores fight over the bone. The wine: Cabernet Sauvignon from California's Napa Valley or Alexander Valley.

Chile-Bourbon Sirloin Steak

Sirloin steak, cut from the hip of the steer, has plenty of flavor, but it can be a bit chewier than fillet or top loin steak. A soak in this Chile-Bourbon Marinade or another spicy marinade will add extra flavor and improve tenderness. The marinade is also delicious on flank steak (see page 142) or skirt steak (see page 142) and can be used with any pork tenderloin recipe (see pages 112, 114, 117). If you marinate pork tenderloin in this or any other acidic marinade, don't leave the pork in the marinade for more than a few hours or it can become mushy.

Chile-Bourbon Marinade

- 3 jalapeño chiles, seeded, and finely chopped
- 1 to 2 ancho chiles, soaked for 30 minutes, drained (reserve ½ cup soaking liquid), seeded, and chopped
- 2 tablespoons dried onion flakes
- 1 tablespoon dried oregano
- ½ cup bourbon
- 1 tablespoon Worcestershire sauce
- 2 tablespoons olive oil
- 2 tablespoons white wine vinegar
- 2 tablespoons chopped garlic
- ½ cup chile soaking liquid

- 2 top sirloin steaks, about 2 pounds each

Make the marinade: In a small bowl, whisk all the ingredients together.

Trim the steaks of external fat. Pour the marinade over the meat in a bowl with a lid or in a resealable plastic bag, making sure the marinade completely covers the steaks. Refrigerate and marinate for up to 12 hours, turning the steaks occasionally, or marinate at room temperature for up to 2 hours. Bring the steaks to room temperature, remove from the marinade, and pat dry before grilling.

Prepare the grill for direct cooking over medium-high heat (350°F). Add mesquite or other hardwood chips or chunks following the directions on page 43.

Sear the steaks over direct heat for 4 to 5 minutes on each side. Move the steaks to a cooler portion of the grill if flare-ups occur. At this point check the internal temperature: Rare is 120°F to 125°F and red at the center; medium-rare is 130°F to 135°F and pink. If the steaks are not done, move them to a cooler portion of the grill to finish cooking. Take the steaks off the grill and let them rest for 5 minutes.

Serve with Campfire Beans (page 150) and Vegetable Mixed Grill (page 181) with a full-bodied red wine from southern France such as Gigondas or Châteauneuf-du-Pape.

New York Strip Steak or Shell Steak with Thyme and Garlic Paste

SERVES 4

Thyme and Garlic Paste

¼ cup chopped fresh thyme or 2 tablespoons dried

4 cloves garlic, chopped

1½ teaspoons salt

1 teaspoon coarsely ground black pepper

Olive oil

4 New York strip steaks, at least 1½
   inches thick, bone-in or boneless

This tasty piece of the beef loin is one of the America's most popular steaks and it is known by many names around the country. On the West Coast it's called a New York steak or New York strip; in the Midwest you'll hear it called a Kansas City steak or hotel steak; in New York a Delmonico or a shell steak. Under any name, it is a delicious cut, tender and juicy, with an intense beef flavor when cooked rare or medium-rare. The herb and garlic paste will help to form a savory crust on the outside of the steak that will keep juices in and add an extra dimension of taste to the meat.

Make the thyme and garlic paste: In a blender, food processor, or mortar, mash together the thyme, garlic, salt, and pepper. Add enough oil to make a paste.

Trim the steaks of most external fat and slash the edges in 1 or 2 places to prevent curling. Rub both sides of the steaks generously with the paste. Wrap the steaks tightly in plastic wrap and refrigerate for up to 12 hours or let sit at room temperature for up to 1 hour. Bring the steaks to room temperature before grilling.

Prepare the grill for direct cooking over medium-high heat (350°F). Add hardwood chips or chunks following directions on page 43.

Grill the steaks over direct heat, turning occasionally, for 8 to 10 minutes total. Move the steaks to a cooler area of the grill if flare-ups occur. Thicker steaks should be moved to a cooler or unheated area of a covered grill to finish cooking to desired temperatures. For rare, remove steaks from the grill when the internal temperature registers 120°F to 125°F; for medium-rare, 130°F to 135°F. Let steaks sit for 5 minutes. Serving with Grilled Portobello Mushrooms (page 190), Smoke-Roasted New Potatoes (page 149), and a full-bodied Australian Shiraz.

Skirt or Flank Steak with Citrus-Chile Marinade

SERVES 4

Citrus-Chile Marinade

2 ancho or other dried chiles or 2 chipotles en adobo

Juice of 1 orange

Juice of 1 lemon

Juice of 1 lime

½ cup olive oil

2 cloves garlic, minced

2 tablespoons molasses

1 tablespoon Worcestershire sauce

1 teaspoon salt

1 teaspoon black pepper

2 pounds skirt steak, cut into 4 serving pieces, or 1 large flank steak (at least 1½ pounds)

Both skirt and flank steak are slightly chewy but very flavorful steaks that gain both tenderness and even more flavor from some time in a tangy marinade. The skirt steak, a long, thin strip of tender beef, is called the fajita or "little belt" in Spanish. It was (and is) a prized cut among Southwest *vaqueros* and cowboys, and when marinated in lime and chiles and sliced thinly, it became the popular fajitas featured on Southwestern restaurant menus. Flank steak is a long-grained muscle from the flank of the steer and is often called London broil when marinated and sliced thinly on the bias against the grain. Both steaks are known for an intense meaty character that takes well to spicy marinades.

Make the marinade: Soak the anchos in hot water to cover for 30 minutes. Drain, then remove and discard the stems and seeds. Put pieces of the soaked chiles with a little soaking water (or the chipotles and a little adobo sauce) in a food processor or blender along with all the other ingredients and process to a coarse puree.

Cut any external fat from the steaks and slash skirt steaks or flank steak across the grain in 2 or 3 places on each side to prevent curling. Pour the marinade over the steaks in a bowl with lid or resealable plastic bag and marinate in the refrigerator for up to 12 hours or marinate for at room temperature for up to 2 hours. Bring the steaks to room temperature before grilling.

Prepare the grill for direct cooking over medium-high heat (350°F). Add mesquite or other hardwood chips or chunks following the directions on page 43.

Grill the steaks over direct heat to the rare (120°F to 125°F) or medium-rare stage (130°F to 135°F). Move the steaks to a cooler part of the grill if flare-ups occur. Skirt steaks should take 3 to 5 minutes per side, a flank steak 5 to 7 minutes per side. Do not overcook them, as skirt or flank steaks become tough if cooked to more than medium-rare. Let steaks rest for 5 minutes. Slice across the grain and serve.

Serve with Grilled Tortillas (page 116), Three-Chile Salsa (page 75), and Campfire Beans (page 150).

The Classic Hamburger with Grilled Onions and the Works

Somehow the hamburger hot from the grill defines American outdoor cooking, and, some would say, American life. Memories of summer afternoons in the backyard with Dad at the barbecue in a cloud of smoke, the family gathering round to build burgers on toasted buns with juicy patties of ground meat, spicy goo, grilled onions, ripe tomatoes, and crisp lettuce are a part of the American dream of the good life. The classic burger is a long way from the fast-food travesties that get served up by the millions every day around the world. The real deal involves good meat that is carefully seasoned and cooked to order, then paired with fresh and tasty ingredients. With a little care, and the right stuff, an old-fashioned American hamburger can make the taste buds rejoice and bring back delicious memories.

Spicy Hamburger Goo

1 cup ketchup

½ cup mayonnaise

¼ cup brown or Dijon mustard

2 tablespoons horseradish

1 tablespoon Worcestershire sauce

Dash of Tabasco or other hot sauce, or more to taste

1 pound ground chuck

Worcestershire sauce

Garlic salt

Coarsely ground black pepper

1 large onion, cut into ½-inch rounds

4 hamburger buns, split

Tomato slices

Iceberg lettuce

Prepare the grill for direct cooking over medium-high heat (350°F). Brush or spray the grill with oil.

Make the Spicy Hamburger Goo: In a small bowl, combine all the ingredients together.

Form the ground meat into 4 patties, about ¾ inch thick. Rub each side with a dash or two of Worcestershire sauce and sprinkle with garlic salt and pepper. Let sit for up to 30 minutes before grilling. Grill the burgers over direct heat, turning from time to time, for 7 to 10 minutes. Move the burgers to a cooler portion of the grill if flare-ups occur. Burgers should be cooked to the well-done stage (160°F) for safety: No pink should be showing inside and the juices should run clear.

Grill the onions over direct heat for 3 to 4 minutes per side, until grill-marked and lightly browned. Do not overcook. Toast the buns, split side down, for 2 to 3 minutes, until lightly browned.

Assemble the burgers: Place a patty on the bottom side of each bun and top with Spicy Hamburger Goo, a slice of tomato, slice of onion and a lettuce leaf. Mash down the top half of the bun. Classic accompaniment? Cold beer.

Carne Asada Tri-Tip

SERVES 6 TO 8

Carne Asada Paste

2 anchos or other dried chiles
(see Chiles, page 60)

1 jalapeño chile, seeded
(see Chiles, page 60)

2 cups chopped grilled tomatoes
(see page 103) chopped fresh or
canned tomatoes

1 cup chopped grilled onions
(see page 89) or ½ cup chopped
raw onions

4 cloves garlic

1 ounce tequila

¼ cup orange juice

½ cup chopped cilantro

2 tablespoons or more tomato paste

2 tablespoons olive oil

½ tablespoon salt

2 (2-pound) beef tri-tips

The tri-tip is a compact, triangular roast cut from the bottom sirloin. It is tender and full of flavor and a great favorite for West Coast grill chefs, especially in California's Santa Maria Valley, where it has become a regional specialty. Santa Maria chefs make a simple rub of garlic salt and black pepper or chile powder, smoke-roast the tri-tip, and serve it with cooked pinto beans. A similar dish could be made using any of our chile-based rubs (pages 94, 150, 153) and Campfire Beans (page 150). Here we put together a spicy marinade often used to make carne asada, chile-accented grilled beef popular throughout the Southwest. The Carne Asada Paste would also be delicious on flank or skirt steak (see page 142) or on pork tenderloins (see pages 112, 114, 117) or pork chops (see page 120).

Make the Carne Asada Paste: Soak the dried chiles in hot water to cover for 30 minutes. Drain, then remove and discard the seeds and stems. Put the chile pieces into a blender or food processor along with the remaining ingredients. Process to a coarse paste, adding more tomato paste if needed to thicken the mixture.

Trim the tri-tips of most external fat and any silverskin, and slash across the grain in 2 or 3 places on each side. Coat the tri-tips well with the paste and wrap tightly in plastic wrap or put them a resealable plastic bag. Refrigerate for up to 12 hours or let sit at room temperature for up to 2 hours. Bring the beef to room temperature before cooking.

Prepare the grill for combination grilling-roasting at medium-high heat (350°F). Brush or spray the grill with oil. Add oak, mesquite, or other hardwood chips following the directions on page 43.

Sear the tri-tips for 4 to 5 minutes per side over direct heat, moving them to a cooler area if flare-ups occur. Cook, covered, for another 10 to 15 minutes on the cooler or unheated part of the grill until done, turning occasionally. For rare, the internal temperature should register 120°F to 125°F and the meat be red at the center; medium-rare should be 130°F to 135°F and pink at the center.

Let the meat rest for 5 to 10 minutes. Carve thinly across the grain and serve with Grilled Corn and Tomato Salsa (page 94) and Campfire Beans (page 150).

Smoke Roasted Tri-Tip with Orange and Chile Glaze

SERVES 4 TO 6 AS A MAIN COURSE

Tri-tip takes well to chile and citrus, and this glaze gives the tasty, tender meat an added kick. You could use this glaze on pork loin roast (see page 128) or pork tenderloins (see pages 112, 114, 117). I use the hot dried chile d'arbol or chipotles here (see Chiles, page 60), but you could substitute ancho or pasilla, which are milder and easier to find. If you use these milder chiles and want a bit more heat, add some Mexican hot sauce such as Tapatio or Bufalo (see Ingredients, page 54) or a few dashes of Tabasco.

1 (2 pound) beef tri-tip

Chile Rub (see pages 94, 150, 153)

Orange and Chile Glaze

1 ancho, pasilla or other dried chile (see Chiles, page 60)

2 chile d'arbol, dried chipotle chiles, or other hot dried chiles (see Chiles, page 60)

3 cups orange juice (preferably freshly squeezed)

¼ cup sweet sherry

1 tablespoon brown sugar

Rub the tri-tip generously with the Chile Rub and let stand at room temperature while you prepare the glaze.

Make the glaze: Soak the dried chiles in hot water to cover for 30 minutes. Drain, reserving the soaking liquid, and remove and discard the stems and seeds and tear the chiles into pieces. Put ¼ cup of the soaking liquid in a blender or food processor along with the dried chiles and puree to a coarse paste. Pour the rest of the soaking water, along with the orange juice, into a saucepan and cook over high heat until the liquid is reduced by half. Add the chile paste, sherry, and brown sugar and simmer for 20 to 30 minutes, stirring often. The glaze should reduce down to a syrupy consistency. Strain the glaze, discarding the solids. You should have ¼ to ½ cup glaze.

Prepare the grill for indirect cooking over medium-high heat (350°F), with a drip pan under the unheated portion of the grill. Add oak or other hardwood chips or chunks following the directions on page 43.

Sear the tri-tip over direct heat for 5 to 7 minutes total, turning often. Brush the meat with the glaze and move it to the unheated portion of the grill over the drip pan. Roast, covered, for another 10 to 20 minutes, depending on the size of the roast and desired doneness. Brush often with the glaze. Take the roast off when the internal temperature registers 125°F for rare, 130°F for medium-rare. Brush again with the glaze and let the meat rest for 5 to 10 minutes. Slice against the grain.

Serve with Grilled Herbed Polenta (page 145) and Sherry Mushroom Gravy (page 144), with a Nebbiolo from Italy's Piedmont area or California.

Herb-Crusted Beef Fillet with Smoke-Roasted New Potatoes

Beef fillet is the most tender part of the steer and is often cut into small, boneless steaks such as filet mignon or tournedos. The fillet also makes a deliciously tender small roast that is especially good when cooked on a smoky grill. Fillet is quite low in fat, however, so care must be taken to not overcook it and to keep it from drying out. A crust of fresh herbs in a garlic-laced paste is a good way to ensure a flavorful exterior and a juicy, tender interior.

5-to 6-pound piece beef fillet

Double-recipe Thyme and Garlic Paste (page 140) or Basil and Garlic Paste (page 86)

Smoke-Roasted New Potatoes

Salt

2 pounds small new potatoes

Olive oil

2 tablespoons dried thyme, rosemary, or oregano

2 tablespoons garlic powder or granulated garlic

2 tablespoons sweet Hungarian or Spanish paprika

1 teaspoon black pepper

Trim any fat or silverskin from the beef and rub well with the herb paste. Wrap the beef tightly in plastic wrap and refrigerate for up to 12 hours or let sit at room temperature for up to an hour before cooking. Bring the beef to room temperature before cooking.

Prepare the grill for indirect cooking over high heat (375°F to 400°F). Brush or spray the grill with oil. Add hardwood chips or chunks following the directions on page 43.

Place the meat on a spit, following the manufacturer's directions, or on the unheated portion of the covered grill over a drip pan. Roast, covered, to desired doneness: 120°F to 125°F for rare, 130°F to 135°F for medium-rare. Start checking the internal temperature after 30 minutes. Remove the meat from the grill and let stand for 10 minutes.

Make the Smoke-Roasted New Potatoes: In plenty of salted water, parboil until the tip of a knife can just be inserted, 5 to 10 minutes, depending on the size. Drain, then toss the potatoes in enough oil to just coat them, then toss with the thyme, garlic powder, paprika, 1½ teaspoons salt, and pepper to coat thoroughly. Grill over direct heat, turning often, until browned and grill-marked, 10 to 15 minutes total.

Slice the beef and serve with the roast potatoes, Vegetable Mixed Grill (page 181), and a full-bodied Cabernet Sauvignon from California, Chile, or Australia.

Roast Sirloin with Southwest Rub and Campfire Beans

SERVES 6 TO 8

Southwest Rub

¼ cup ancho chile powder or blended chili powder, preferably Gebhardt

1 tablespoon chipotle powder or blended chili powder, preferably Gebhardt

1 tablespoon dried sage

1 tablespoon dried oregano

1 tablespoon dried cilantro

2 tablespoons brown sugar

2 tablespoons garlic powder

1 teaspoon ground allspice

½ tablespoon salt

1 teaspoon black pepper

1 (4-to 5-pound) beef sirloin or shoulder roast, rolled and tied

Campfire Beans

1 pound dried pinto beans or 4 cups canned

2 ancho or other dried chiles

2 cups chopped grilled tomatoes (see page 103) or chopped fresh or canned tomatoes

3 cloves garlic

½ cup barbecue sauce, homemade or store bought

1 onion, chopped

1 red bell pepper, chopped

¼ cup Southwest Rub or other chile-based spice rub

1 cup or more water or tomato juice as needed

Salt and hot sauce to taste

This is a version of a cowboy campfire staple: beef and beans cooked over the coals. Cowboys used a Dutch oven tucked right into the coals or hung over the fire, but we prefer a kettle barbecue with the beef roasted in wood smoke over indirect heat and the beans cooked in a Dutch oven or foil-covered pan. The Southwest Rub can be used wherever you want a spicy, chile flavor on grilled meat or poultry.

Make the Southwest Rub: In a small bowl, mix all the ingredients together.

Sprinkle the rub all over the beef roast. Wrap the roast tightly with plastic wrap and refrigerate for up to 12 hours or let the roast sit at room temperature for up to 2 hours. Bring the meat to room temperature before cooking.

Make the Campfire Beans: If using dried beans, cover the beans with water in a Dutch oven or ovenproof saucepan and bring to a boil. Cover, turn off the heat, and let the beans sit for 1 hour. Drain and discard the water, cover with water again, and cook, covered, over low heat until done, 2 to 3 hours; drain. If using canned pinto beans, drain and rinse in cold water. Use about 4 cups drained, canned beans (be careful with salt levels if you use canned beans). Soak the dried chiles in hot water to cover for 30 minutes. Drain, then remove and discard the stems and seeds and tear the chiles into pieces. Place the chiles in a blender or food processor along with the tomatoes, garlic, and barbecue sauce. Process to a coarse puree. In the Dutch oven, combine the beans, puree, onion, bell pepper, Southwest Rub, and 1 cup water or tomato juice. Cover the pot.

Prepare the grill for indirect cooking over medium-low heat (300°F to 325°F), with a drip pan under the unheated portion of the grill. Add hickory, oak, mesquite, or other hardwood chips or chunks following the directions on page 43.

POTATOES ON THE GRILL

Potatoes cooked over the grill take on a lovely smoky flavor that ties them in to the food you've been grilling. My gas grill comes with a handy rack inside the cover that can fit 6 to 8 baking potatoes, but you can place potatoes anywhere on the unheated portion of a kettle grill. While you are cooking the main course over indirect heat, the potatoes bake along with it. I use russet or Idaho potatoes for baking and usually prepare more than I need for dinner. Baked potatoes keep for a week or so in the refrigerator, and I chop them and fry them with onions, garlic, and herbs for delicious home fries (see Leftovers, page 84). You can also make smoke-roasted new potatoes over direct heat. Simply boil for 5 to 10 minutes, coat with oil and spices, and grill until brown (see page 149).

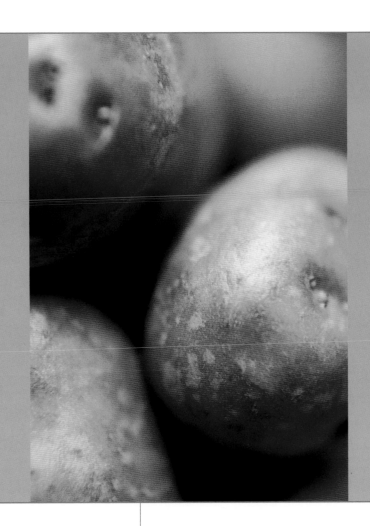

Put the beef roast over the drip pan on the unheated part of the grill and put the Dutch oven with the beans, on another part of the unheated section. Cook, covered, for 30 minutes. Check the beans: They should be simmering and still have enough liquid to keep from sticking. Add more water or tomato juice, if needed. Continue to cook until the roast is done, 30 minutes or more, until the internal temperature registers 120°F to 125°F for rare, 130°F to 135°F for medium-rare. Check the beans for salt and heat levels.

Let the beef rest for 10 minutes. Slice and serve with the beans and Grilled Corn with Chile-Garlic Butter (page 191). The drink of choice: Lone Star or Shiner beer from Texas.

Rib Roast with Mustard and Herb Crust

SERVES 6 TO 8

1 (5-to 6-pound) rib roast, bone-in or boneless, or a (6-to 7-pound) bone-in standing rib roast

Mustard and Herb Paste

½ cup Dijon mustard

¼ cup chopped fresh thyme or 2 tablespoons dried

¼ cup chopped fresh rosemary or 2 tablespoons dried

6 cloves garlic, chopped

2 tablespoons soy sauce

1 teaspoon coarsely ground black pepper

A rib roast is a sumptuous cut of beef from the loin that is often called standing rib roast, prime rib, or rib-eye roast. You can cook it with the bone still in or as a boneless roast. If you are using a rotisserie, the boneless roast will balance better on the spit, but the bone-in roast can be used as well. This smoky, tender beef makes some of the best roast beef sandwiches, hot or cold, that I've ever tasted. The Mustard and Herb Paste is also very tasty on rack of lamb (see page 167) or pork tenderloin (see pages 112, 114, 117).

Make the Mustard and Herb Paste: In a small bowl, mix all the ingredients together.

Trim most external fat from the outside of the roast. Rub the paste liberally all over the meat. Wrap the roast tightly in plastic wrap and refrigerate overnight or let sit at room temperature for up to 2 hours. Bring the meat to room temperature before cooking.

Prepare the grill for spit-roasting or indirect cooking over medium-high heat (350°F), with a drip pan under the unheated portion of the grill. Add oak, hickory, or other hardwood chips or chunks following the directions on page 43.

Attach the roast to the spit following the manufacturer's directions and page 48, or place it over the drip pan on the unheated portion of the grill. Roast, covered, until done to your liking. Begin checking the meat after about 45 minutes: For rare, the internal temperature should register 120°F to 125°F and the roast should be red at the center; medium-rare should be 130°F to 135°F and pink at the center. Continue cooking to desired temperature, about another hour or more. Let the meat rest for 10 to 15 minutes. The internal temperature will rise 5°F to 10°F as the meat rests.

Carve the roast and serve with Smoke-Baked Potatoes (page 151) and Roasted Garlic (page 159) and Grilled Portobello Mushrooms (page 190). Syrah from California or southern France is a good choice here.

Pit-Roasted Beef Shoulder, Asadero Style

SERVES 4 AS A MAIN COURSE, 8 TO 10 ON SANDWICHES

Southwest pit barbecue cooks roast chile-rubbed beef shoulder in hot, smoky firepits to the medium-rare to medium stage with great results. They're following the lead of the asaderos, Mexican and Texan cooks who would wrap and bury chunks of beef underneath a bed of hot coals and let them roast overnight. A beef shoulder roast or a rolled boneless chuck roast is a good cut to use here. Don't worry about leftovers, as you'll be serving some of the best barbecued beef sandwiches around if you reheat beef slices in your favorite barbecue sauce.

Ancho Chile Rub

2 tablespoons ancho chile powder or blended chili powder, such as Gebhardt

1 tablespoon ground cumin

1 tablespoon dry mustard

1 tablespoon onion powder

1 tablespoon garlic powder

1 tablespoon dried oregano

½ tablespoon salt

1 teaspoon black pepper

1 (3- to 5-pound) beef shoulder roast

Make the chile rub: In a small bowl, mix all the ingredients together.

Coat the roast generously with the chile rub, wrap in plastic wrap, and refrigerate for up to 12 hours or let sit for at room temperature up to 2 hours. Bring the roast to room temperature before cooking.

Method I: Long, Slow Cooking

In an offset smoker-cooker, start 8 to 10 charcoal briquettes in the fire-box (see Offset Smoker-Cooker, page 46). When the coals are gray, add hardwood chips or chunks, using both soaked and dry chips to achieve a temperature between 200°F and 225°F. Put the meat in the smoker-cooker and smoke for 4 to 5 hours. When the shoulder reaches an internal temperature of 135°F, or medium-rare, take it out of the smoker and let it rest for at least 10 minutes.

Method II: Indirect Cooking

Prepare the grill for indirect cooking over medium-high heat (350°F), with a drip pan under the unheated portion of the grill. Add hardwood chips or chunks following the directions on page 43. Place the roast on the unheated portion of the grill and smoke-roast to the medium-rare stage. Start checking the internal temperature after 1 hour. When the internal temperature reaches 135°F, or medium rare, remove the roast and let it rest for at least 10 minutes.

Carve the roast and serve with Three-Chile Salsa (page 75) and Grilled Corn with Chile-Garlic Butter (page 191).

Texas-Style Brisket

SERVES 10 TO 12 AS A MAIN COURSE, A LARGE PARTY ON SANDWICHES

Chile Rub (see pages 94, 150, or 153)

Vinegar-Chile Mop (page 123) or your favorite barbecue sauce (optional)

1 (10-to-12-pound) untrimmed brisket

Brisket is a tough but extremely tasty cut from the belly area of the steer. It needs long, slow roasting to become lusciously tender and absolutely delicious. Texas pit roasters have brought brisket to perfection. They like to rub it with a lively mix of spices and roast it for 8, 10, 12, or more hours in a slow and smoky fire. My nephew Jeff Clark is one of those patient barbecue cooks and he has given us a recipe (Method I) for cooking brisket in an offset smoker-cooker, which is used to maintain very low temperatures over many hours (see Offset Smoker-Cooker, page 46). We've also provided a quicker method, which gives good results in about 3 hours in a kettle grill. Refer to the section on Long, Slow Cooking (page 37) for more information. Try to find an untrimmed (that is, with a thick cap of fat) brisket, as you'll get juicer results if you cook the brisket with the fat cap on and remove it just before you slice the cooked meat. Ask the butcher for an untrimmed brisket with the fat cap and deckle still on or a whole packer's cut brisket.

Method I: Long, Slow Cooking

In an offset smoker-cooker, start 8 to 10 charcoal briquettes in the firebox (see Offset Smoker-Cooker, page 46). When the coals turn gray, add hardwood chunks or chips, using both soaked and dry wood to achieve a temperature between 200°F and 225°F, in the smoker box. Place the brisket on the grill in a disposable drip pan or on a rimmed baking sheet. Smoke the roast at this low temperature for 8 to 10 hours, turning the brisket every hour. After the first 6 hours, generously baste every 30 minutes with Vinegar-Chile Mop or your favorite barbecue sauce, if you wish, making sure to incorporate any drippings from the pan. When the brisket reaches an internal temperature of 150°F to 180°F and is very tender, remove it from the grill, wrap it in heavy-duty foil, and let rest for at least 30 minutes.

Method II: Indirect Cooking

Prepare a kettle grill for indirect grilling over low heat (250°F to 275°F) (see page 40). Place the brisket on the unheated portion of the grill in a disposable drip pan, and

FAMILY PARTY SALADS

My extended family extends quite a bit, and we love to party outdoors at the beach or in backyard gardens with ribs or steaks or chicken hot off the grill and big bowls of peppery coleslaw and tangy potato salad. Here are a couple of family favorites from my sisters, Kathy Clark and Janet Schultz, both great cooks who love a party.

Kathy's Jalapeño Coleslaw

1 head cabbage, shredded	1 teaspoon celery seed
1 cup sugar	1 jalapeño chile, seeded and
1 large onion, chopped	finely chopped
1 cup apple cider vinegar	Salt and pepper to taste
¾ cup vegetable oil	

In a large bowl, layer the cabbage, sugar, and onion. Do not stir. In a nonreactive saucepan, bring the vinegar, oil, celery seed, and chile to a boil. Remove from the heat and pour over the cabbage and onion mixture. Cover the bowl and refrigerate overnight to marinate. Before serving, stir the slaw well and remove with a slotted spoon to a serving bowl or plate. Taste for salt and pepper.

Jan's Seaside Potato Salad

5 pounds red new potatoes, skin on	6 green onions, white and green parts, chopped
2 or 3 whole dill pickles, diced	1 cup mayonnaise
1 tablespoon dill pickle juice	¼ cup ranch dressing
½ cup chopped fresh dill	¼ cup sour cream
6 hard-cooked eggs, 5 chopped, 1 sliced	1 tablespoon Dijon mustard
3 ribs celery, finely diced	Salt and pepper

Cook the potatoes in boiling salted water to cover until just barely done. Let cool, then cut into bite-size pieces. In a large bowl, combine the potatoes with the pickles, pickle juice, dill (reserve a little for garnish), chopped eggs (reserve the sliced egg for garnish), celery, and green onions. In a small bowl, stir together the mayonnaise, ranch dressing, sour cream, and mustard and stir the mixture into the potato and vegetable mixture. The salad should be quite moist. Add more mayonnaise as needed. Taste for salt and pepper. Garnish the top with the reserved dill and sliced eggs.

cover with foil. Let it roast, covered, for 1½ hours. Unwrap the meat and add plenty of hardwood chips or chunks to the fire following the directions on page 43. Smoke-roast the meat for another 1½ hours or until the brisket is very tender basting every thirty minutes with the Vinegar-Chile Mop or your favorite barbecue sauce. Remove it from the grill, and wrap it in heavy-duty foil and let it rest for at least 30 minutes.

Serve the brisket in thick slices cut across the grain, with barbecue sauce, if you wish, and Kathy's Jalapeño Coleslaw and Jan's Seaside Potato Salad.

Clarks' Smoky Brisket

SERVES 4 AS A MAIN COURSE, 8 TO 10 FOR SANDWICHES

Chris Clark's Marinade for Brisket

½ pound thick-sliced bacon, cut into chunks

1 large onion, diced

5 cloves garlic, diced

1 (12-ounce) can lager beer

1 (6-ounce) can tomato paste

¼ cup molasses

¼ cup packed brown sugar

1 teaspoon cayenne

2 sprigs fresh thyme or 1 teaspoon dried

2 bay leaves

½ tablespoon salt

1 teaspoon black pepper

1 (3-to 5-pound) piece brisket

Jeff and Chris Clark, my nephews, and their father, John Clark, often get together at John's place up in the foothills of California's Sierras to do some heavy-duty barbecuing. Over many smoky afternoons they have come up with ways of cooking brisket that keeps it juicy and tender while adding spicy undertones to the smoky meat. Here's Chris Clark's garlicky marinade for brisket. In this recipe, a half brisket, easier to find than the untrimmed, whole brisket, is used to provide the centerpiece for a family barbecue or plenty of sandwiches for a yardful of friends and neighbors.

Make the marinade: In a skillet over medium heat, render the fat from the bacon and remove the bacon to a paper towel–lined plate. Sauté the onion and garlic in the bacon fat for 4 to 5 minutes, until soft and transparent. Stir in the tomato paste and cook for 3 to 4 minutes, stirring often, to carmelize the onions lightly. Pour in the beer to deglaze the pan, then stir in the remaining ingredients. Simmer the marinade for about 1 hour over low heat until the mixture is the consistency of ketchup. Let the marinade cool. Pour the marinade over the brisket in a bowl with lid or in a resealable plastic bag and marinate in the refrigerator for up to 12 hours or at room temperature for up to 2 hours. Bring the brisket to room temperature before grilling.

Method I: Long, Slow Cooking

In an offset smoker-cooker, start 8 to 10 charcoal briquettes in the fire-box (see Offset Smoker-Cooker, page 46). When the coals turn gray, add hardwood chunks or chips, using both soaked and dry wood to achieve a temperature between 200°F to 225°F, following the directions on page 37. Place the brisket on the grill in a disposable drip pan with the marinade or on a rimmed baking sheet. Smoke the roast at this low temperature for 4 to 6 hours, turning the brisket over every hour. After the first 3 hours, baste every 30 minutes with the marinade and any drippings in the pan. When the brisket reaches an internal temperature of 150°F to 180°F and is very tender, remove it from the grill, wrap it in heavy-duty foil, and let it rest for at least 20 minutes.

ROASTED GARLIC

I often roast 3 or 4 heads of garlic in my covered grill when I am cooking a bird or large piece of meat by indirect heat. I figure that while I have the barbecue fired up for a while, I might as well take advantage of all that heat and roast some garlic. When the garlic is done, I'll use one head in a sauce or with the meat or poultry, and save the others in the fridge for later use in an aïoli or other garlicky sauce. Roasting garlic is simple: Slice off the top ¼ or ½ inch of the unpeeled head of garlic with a serrated knife. Brush or spray with oil a square of heavy-duty foil big enough to enclose the head; wrap the garlic in the foil; and bake it on a rack or an unheated spot in a covered kettle grill for about 1 hour at medium-high heat. The garlic is done when the cloves are soft and can be squeezed out.

Method II: Indirect Cooking

Prepare a kettle grill for indirect cooking over low heat (250°F to 300°F) (see page 40). Place the brisket with the marinade in a disposable drip pan, on the unheated portion of the grill and cover with heavy-duty foil. Cook the roast, covered, for 1 hour. Uncover and add plenty of hardwood chips or chunks following the directions on page 43. Smoke-roast the meat for another 1 to 1½ hours, or until the brisket is very tender, basting with the marinade and drippings in the pan from time to time. Remove from the grill, wrap the brisket in heavy-duty foil, and let it rest for at least 20 minutes.

Serve the brisket in thick slices cut across the grain, with barbecue sauce, if you wish, and Campfire Beans (page 150).

Cow-Country
Dutch Oven Short Ribs

SERVES 4 TO 6

Chile Rub (pages 94, 150, or 153)

4 to 5 pounds short ribs, cut into
1½-inch pieces

2 anchos or other dried chiles
(See Chiles, page 60)

2 cups chopped grilled tomatoes
(see page 103) or chopped fresh
or canned tomatoes

4 cloves garlic

1 onion, peeled and chopped

3 bay leaves

1 (12-ounce) bottle or more dark beer

1 cup barbecue sauce, homemade or
store-bought

Salt and pepper to taste

Short Ribs have a very beefy flavor, more intense than any other part of the steer. They are, however, cut from well-used muscles along the bottom of the ribs and need long, slow cooking to become luscious and tender. Grilling the ribs on a smoky fire and then braising them with a chile-laced sauce in a Dutch oven or foil-wrapped pan brings these savory ribs to perfection. They pick up the smoke from the smoldering wood and become falling-off-the-bone tender after long, slow cooking in the spicy braise. They make delicious tacos or burritos (see Tacos and Burritos, page 176) and are wonderful spooned over soft grits or polenta.

Trim the short ribs of most external fat and rub the ribs thoroughly with the chile rub. Wrap tightly in plastic wrap or put into resealable plastic bags and refrigerate for up to 12 hours or let sit at room temperature for up to 1 hour. Bring the ribs to room temperature before cooking.

Soak the dried chiles in warm water to cover for 30 minutes. Drain, then remove and discard the stems and seeds and tear the chiles into pieces. In a blender or food processor, puree the chiles together with the tomatoes, garlic, and onion. Combine the chile puree in a Dutch oven or heavy-duty foil pan with the bay leaves, beer, and barbecue sauce. Taste the braising liquid for salt and pepper. Keep the salt level on the low side to compensate for salt in the rub; you can taste for salt again when the dish is finished.

Prepare the grill for indirect cooking over medium heat (300°F to 325°F). Add hardwood chips or chunks following the directions on page 43.

Grill the short ribs over direct heat in the wood smoke for 10 to 12 minutes, turning often, until grill-marked and nicely browned. Place them in the braising liquid, cover the Dutch oven or cover the foil pan tightly with heavy-duty foil, and put on the unheated portion of the grill. Bake, covered, for 2 hours or more. Add more beer if necessary. Test for doneness: The meat should be very tender and almost falling off the bones. If not, continue to cook until tender. Skim any fat from the top of the braising liquid and taste again for salt.

Serve the short ribs with Campfire Beans (page 150) and Grilled Tortillas (page 116) along with the same beer you added to the braise.

Lamb

There is a long tradition of grilling lamb on the fire in the Mediterranean: I remember visiting villages in the mountains near Delphi when I lived in Greece and seeing ten or fifteen whole lambs stretched on spits over coals at festivals. Garlicky leg of lamb, grilled over wood fires, is a specialty in southern France. Americans have not accepted lamb as a food for grilling the way they have steak or pork. But in recent years the influence of Mediterranean and, in the West, Basque cooking has made grilled lamb a part of the modern grill cook's repertoire.

When I cook lamb on the grill, I think of the delicious grilled lamb I've eaten in Greece, Provence, and in the many Basque restaurants and hotels that serve hungry sheep herders in Western states. The seasonings here are traditional: garlic, lemon, rosemary, oregano, and other savory herbs. Another influence on

FLAVORED OILS

Olive or vegetable oil, flavored with herbs, garlic, and/or spices, makes a welcome addition to salads, sauces, or on grilled vegetables, meat, poultry, or fish. There are quite a number of very tasty flavored oils in markets these days, from inexpensive American garlic and herb oils to very pricey flavored Italian olive oils in fancy bottles. I use these commercial flavored oils or, often, I make my own. Making flavored oil in a blender or food processor is easy: Blend together 2 cups of olive or vegetable oil with about 2 tablespoons fresh chopped herb leaves (basil, thyme, rosemary, sage, and so on) with a garlic clove or two, the juice of ½ lemon, and salt to taste. Use the oil as is or strain before using. I don't think it's a good idea to try to store these homemade herb and garlic oils. The herbs can discolor and the garlic can get rancid if you try to keep them for any length of time. I just make them up for the recipe, and use whatever is left on a salad served with the main course.

modern grillers of lamb are Asian flavors such as black beans, chile, and soy, which provide spicy undertones to lamb's slightly gamy flavor.

Lamb chops are easy to grill and make a great appetizer or main course. Small rib chops or larger loin chops can both be cooked quickly over medium-high heat to the rare or medium-rare stage. Rack of lamb, with 7 or 8 rib chops, makes an ideal small roast for an elegant dinner party for two. Most racks are "frenched" before cooking by cutting out the fat and connective tissue between the rib bones, and then seared over high heat and roasted in medium-high heat until done.

Leg of lamb, usually butterflied to make a flat piece of tender meat, can be easily cooked by combination grilling-roasting. Season the meat with plenty of garlic, oregano, and lemon and stabilize it with skewers for easy handling. I cook leg of lamb to the medium-rare stage, but cook it to your own preference. Lamb shoulder, slightly chewier and with more fat than the leg, is best spit-roasted or roasted over indirect heat; it can be boned and stuffed before roasting.

Rack of Lamb with Black Bean–Garlic Crust, recipe on page 167

Lamb Lollipops: Rib Chops with Roast Garlic Aïoli

SERVES 6 AS AN APPETIZER, 4 AS A MAIN COURSE

12 lamb rib chops

Spicy Asian Marinade

¼ cup tamari or soy sauce

1 teaspoon of Asian hot chile oil,
  or more to taste

4 cloves garlic, minced

Lemon pepper

Roast Garlic Aïoli

1 egg

4 cloves roast garlic (see page 159)

Juice of ½ lemon

Dash of Asian hot chile oil,
  or more to taste

1 teaspoon lemon pepper

1 cup olive oil

Salt to taste

Tiny, succulent lamb rib chops with the bones frenched make fantastic appetizers or elegant party food when paired with a tangy sauce like Roast Garlic Aïoli. You can ask the butcher to french the chops or do them yourself. Asian hot chile oil is available in most markets (see Ingredients, page 54) or by mail order (see Sources, page 200). Use as much or as little as your want, depending on your heat tolerance. The Spicy Asian Marinade is also good with rack of lamb and on steak.

French the rib chops by cutting away all connective tissue and meat from the rib bone all the way down to the nugget of meat on each chop. The rib bone thus becomes the handle of the "lollipop."

Make the marinade: In a small bowl, mix together the tamari, Asian hot chile oil, and garlic and brush the marinade on both sides of the meat of all the chops. Sprinkle both sides of the chops with lemon pepper. Wrap the chops tightly in plastic wrap and refrigerate for up to 12 hours or let sit at room temperature for up to 2 hours. Bring the lamb to room temperature before cooking.

Prepare the grill for direct cooking over high heat (375°F to 400°F). Brush or spray the grill with oil. Add hardwood chips or chunks following the directions on page 43.

Grill the chops over direct heat, turning often, for 3 to 4 minutes per side, until done. Move them to a cooler area of the grill if flare-ups occur. The internal temperature of rare lamb should register 125°F, medium-rare 135°F.

Make the aïoli: Place the egg in a blender or food processor along with the garlic, lemon juice, Asian hot chile oil, and lemon pepper. Gradually add the oil in a thin stream with the blender or processor running until the aïoli is emulsified. Add salt to taste.

Serve the chops right off the grill with the aïoli as a dip, with a fragrant rosé from southern France such as Tavel. For a main course, serve the chops with the aïoli and Smoked Tomato Risotto (page 96) along with a Pinot Noir from Oregon.

Basque Sheep Herder's Skewered Lamb

Some of the best lamb I've ever eaten has been in restaurants and hotels that cater to the Basque sheep herders who tend their flocks in the rugged countryside of Nevada and California. Huge platters of roast leg of lamb, grilled chops, or skewers of tender lamb flavored with garlic, herbs, and peppers are put on the tables, and hungry diners help themselves. Washed down with pitchers of hearty red wine and paired with lively conversation and a few songs, dinner at a Basque table is an unforgettable experience. The Red Wine Marinade is also delicious with lamb chops, butterflied leg of lamb, and beef tri-tip, flank steak, or skirt steak. If you can, use smoked Spanish paprika and a Spanish dried chile such as choricero, available in some specialty stores or by mail order (see Sources, page 200).

Red Wine Marinade

- 1 ancho, choricero, or other dried chile
- 2 cups chopped grilled tomatoes (see page 103), or chopped fresh, or canned tomatoes
- ¼ cup red wine
- 2 tablespoons red wine vinegar
- 2 tablespoons olive oil
- 6 cloves garlic
- 1 onion, coarsely chopped
- 1 red bell pepper, coarsely chopped
- 2 tablespoons sweet smoked Spanish or other paprika
- 1 tablespoon hot smoked Spanish or other paprika
- 1 teaspoon salt
- 1 teaspoon black pepper

- 2 pounds leg or shoulder of lamb, cut into 1½-inch cubes

Make the Red Wine Marinade: Soak the chile in hot water to cover for 30 minutes. Drain, then remove and discard the stems and seeds. Put the chile in a blender or food processor along with the rest of the ingredients. Process to a coarse puree.

Pour the marinade over the lamb in a bowl with a lid or in a resealable plastic bag and marinate in the refrigerator for up to 12 hours or marinate at room temperature for up to 2 hours. Bring the lamb to room temperature before cooking.

Prepare the grill for direct cooking over medium-high heat (350°F). Add mesquite or other hardwood chips or chunks following the directions on page 43.

Remove the lamb pieces from the marinade and pat dry. Thread the cubes onto skewers. Grill over direct heat for 8 to 10 minutes, turning often, until the lamb is done. Move the skewers to a cooler area of the grill if flare-ups occur. Test with a meat thermometer or by cutting a cube: Rare lamb should register 125°F and be red at the center; medium-rare should be 135°F and pink.

Serve the lamb skewers with Grilled Herb Polenta (page 145). A southern red wine from France such as Madiran or Coteaux du Languedoc would taste good with the lamb.

Lamb and Pepper Skewers
with Adobo Rice

SERVES 4

2 pounds lamb leg or shoulder, cut into
   1½-inch cubes

2 red or yellow bell peppers, cut into 1½-
   inch pieces

½ cup Chipotle Adobo (page 119)

2 tablespoons vegetable oil

1 tablespoon lemon juice

Salt and pepper

Adobo Rice

¼ cup Chipotle Adobo (page 119)

1 cup or more chicken stock

1 cup chopped grilled tomatoes
   (see page 103) or chopped fresh or
   canned tomatoes

1 teaspoon salt

½ teaspoon black pepper

1 cup long-grain rice

This recipe uses the Chipotle Adobo from Pork Loin Chops Adobado (page 000) to give these lamb skewers and the accompanying rice a Southwest flavor of smoked chiles, tomatoes, and garlic. You could vary the flavors by substituting one of the Grilled Tomato Sauces (pages 182–83) or by using your favorite tomato sauce in place of the adobo.

Thread the lamb and pepper pieces alternately onto skewers. In a small bowl, mix together the adobo, oil, and lemon juice and brush generously on all sides of the lamb and peppers. Let the skewers sit at room temperature while you make the rice.

Make the rice: In a covered saucepan, bring the adobo, stock, tomatoes, salt, and pepper to a boil. Stir in the rice, cover, and cook over low for 20 minutes, or until the rice is tender and all the liquid is absorbed. If you need more liquid, add more stock.

Prepare the grill for direct cooking over medium-high heat (350°F). Brush or spray the grill with oil. Add hardwood chips or chunks following the directions on page 43.

Grill the lamb and pepper skewers over direct heat for about 10 minutes, turning often, until the lamb is done. Move the skewers to a cooler part of the grill if flare-ups occur. Baste the skewers with any leftover adobo as they cook. Test the meat with a meat thermometer or by cutting into a cube: Rare lamb should register 125°F and be red at the center, medium-rare should be 135°F and pink.

Serve the lamb and peppers on the Adobo Rice with Eggplant Grilled in Oregano Smoke (page 178). A medium-bodied red wine such as Spanish Rioja would make a good match.

Rack of Lamb with Black Bean–Garlic Crust

Pictured on page 163   SERVES 4

A rack of lamb is ideal for two people and, when grilled, it makes an elegant and dramatic centerpiece for an outdoor summer supper. Most racks are frenched before cooking: The connective tissue, fat, and meat is removed from between the rib bones down to about an inch from the tender meat. You can easily do this yourself, or have the butcher do it for you. New Zealand and Australian lamb racks are usually sold frenched, tightly wrapped in Cryovac. In this recipe, Black Bean–Garlic Paste gives the lamb a spicy Asian character. Chinese black bean and garlic sauce, made with fermented black beans, is available in many supermarkets, Asian groceries, and by mail order (see Sources, page 200). You could also use one of the many fresh herb pastes in the book (pages 86, 140, or 170) with rack of lamb.

Black Bean–Garlic Paste

- ¼ cup Chinese black bean and garlic sauce
- 2 cloves garlic, minced
- Juice of 1 lime
- 2 tablespoons tamari or soy sauce
- 2 tablespoons sweet sherry
- 1 teaspoon Asian hot chile oil, or more to taste
- 2 racks of lamb (about 7 to 8 ribs per rack), chine bone removed

French the racks by removing the fat, connective tissue, and meat from between the rib bones down to about an inch from the nugget of meat. Remove and discard most external fat.

In a small bowl, mix together the ingredients for the Black Bean–Garlic Paste and spread it all over the lamb. Wrap meat tightly in plastic wrap and refrigerate for up to 12 hours or let sit at room temperature for up to 2 hours. Bring the lamb to room temperature before cooking.

Prepare the grill for combination grilling-roasting at high heat (375°F to 400°F). Brush or spray the grill with oil. Add hardwood chips or chunks following the directions on page 000.

Sear the lamb racks on all sides for 7 to 8 minutes, turning often. Move the lamb to an unheated or cooler portion of the grill and continue cooking until desired doneness: 125°F interior temperature for rare, 135°F for medium-rare, 140°F for medium. Start checking the lamb after 30 minutes on the grill. Let the racks rest for 5 minutes and remove the foil from the bones. Carve into chops and serve with Sweet and Sour Rice (page 69).

Butterflied Leg of Lamb with Ginger-Mustard Crust

SERVES 6 TO 8

Ginger-Mustard Paste

½ cup Dijon mustard

¼ cup chopped fresh oregano or
   2 tablespoons dried

2 tablespoons chopped ginger

4 cloves garlic, minced

Juice of 2 lemons

2 tablespoons tamari or soy sauce

2 tablespoons Hungarian or
   Spanish sweet paprika

1 tablespoon lemon pepper

1 (5-to-7-pound) boned, butterflied
   leg of lamb

A butterflied leg of lamb with a savory crust is a perfect dish for a large dinner party or summer buffet. Butterflying the lamb makes it easy to cook on the grill, and the different thicknesses of meat ensure that you'll have lamb cooked to everybody's liking. You can buttterfly the lamb yourself (see below) or have your butcher do it. I think it's a good idea to stabilize and shape the meat using two long metal skewers so that you can handle the butterflied leg more easily on the grill. Any of the herb pastes in this book (see pages 86, 140, 170) will also work well in this recipe, and the Ginger-Mustard Paste is also good on beef.

Make the Ginger-Mustard Paste: In a small bowl, mix all the ingredients together.

Have the butcher bone and butterfly the leg of lamb or do it yourself by cutting out the thigh bone (and hip bone if attached) from the cut side of the leg, spreading the lamb out fat side down, and then cutting through and flattening the thicker parts of the meat to make the whole piece as flat as you can.

Trim any excess fat and fell from the lamb. Run long metal skewers crosswise through the meat to keep it flat. Rub all sides of the lamb with the paste. Wrap tightly in plastic wrap and refrigerate for up to 12 hours or let sit at room temperature for up to 2 hours. Bring the lamb to room temperature before cooking.

Prepare the grill for indirect cooking over medium-high heat (350°F), with a drip pan under the unheated portion of the grill. Brush or spray the grill with oil. Add hardwood chips or chunks following the directions on page 43.

Sear the lamb over direct heat for 4 to 5 minutes per side, moving it to a cooler area of the grill if flare-ups occur. Put the lamb on the unheated portion of the grill over the drip pan and cook for 20 to 30 minutes, until done, turning it occasionally. Test with a meat thermometer in the thickest part of the lamb: 125°F and red at the center is rare, 135°F and pink at the center is medium-rare. Cook longer if necessary. Let the lamb rest for 5 minutes. Remove the skewers, carve across the grain, and serve with Vegetable Mixed Grill (page 181) and Cabernet Sauvignon from Australia or France's Bordeaux region.

Boned, Stuffed Leg of Lamb, Spit-Roasted with Mint, Chile, and Vinegar Mop

SERVES 6 TO 8

Stuffing a boned leg of lamb with fresh herbs, chile, and garlic gives you meat with plenty of flavor, and basting with a chile- and herb-infused mop provides a beautifully browned and delectable exterior. A double recipe of any of the fresh herb pastes in this book (pages 86, 140, 170), generously rubbed inside and outside the boned leg of lamb, would also be delicious. Use the rotissserie attachment, if you have one, or roast the lamb by indirect heat in a kettle grill. Have the butcher bone the lamb for you or do it yourself, following the directions below.

1 (5-to-7-pound) leg of lamb

Salt and pepper

Mint, Oregano, and Chipotle Stuffing

1½ cups chopped mint

1½ cups chopped oregano

2 chipotles en adobo (see Chiles page 60), chopped

6 cloves garlic, chopped

Adobo from chipotles

Mint, Chile, and Vinegar Mop

1 cup white wine

½ cup white wine vinegar

½ cup chopped fresh mint

4 chipotles en adobo, chopped

½ tablespoon salt

1 bunch mint for mopping (optional)

Have the butcher bone the lamb for you, or bone it yourself by cutting out the thigh bone (and hip bone if attached) from the cut side of the leg and spreading the meat out, skin side down. If the butcher has tied the roast, remove the strings and lay the meat out, skin side down. Sprinkle salt and pepper liberally on both sides of the lamb. Remove and discard exterior fat and fell.

Make the stuffing: In a small bowl, mix all the stuffing ingredients together and spread it liberally on the cut side of the meat. Roll the lamb leg up and tie it in 3 or 4 places. Brush the outside liberally with adobo from the chipotles.

Make the Mint, Chile, and Vinegar Mop: In a large bowl or pan, mix all the ingredients together.

Prepare the grill for spit-roasting, following the manufacturer's directions and page 000, or for indirect cooking over medium-high heat (350°F). Add hardwood chips or chunks following the directions on page 43.

Arrange the lamb on a spit, following the manufacturer's directions and page 48, or position it above a drip pan on the unheated part of the grill.

Spit-roast or cook the lamb over indirect heat, basting the meat often as it cooks with the mop, using a brush, a clean dish mop, or a bunch of mint. Cook until the internal temperature reaches 125°F for rare, 135°F for medium-rare, or 140°F for medium. Start checking the interior temperature of the meat at its thickest part after 1 hour. Remove the lamb from the grill and let rest for 10 minutes before removing the strings and carving the roast.

Lamb Chops with Mint, Tomato, and Onion Relish

SERVES 4

Rosemary-Mint Paste

¼ cup chopped rosemary or
  2 tablespoons dried

¼ cup chopped mint

4 cloves garlic, chopped

½ tablespoon salt

1 teaspoon black pepper

Olive oil

12 rib lamb chops or 8 loin lamb chops

Mint, Tomato, and Onion Relish

½ cup chopped mint

3 cups chopped tomatoes

1 cup chopped sweet onion
  (Maui, Walla Walla, Vidalia)

Juice of 1 lemon

1 tablespoon sherry vinegar or
  white wine vinegar

¼ cup olive oil

Salt and pepper to taste

Lamb chops are at their best when cooked briefly over a smoky fire. Rosemary and mint are herbs that go beautifully with lamb, but you could also use thyme, oregano, or marjoram in this recipe. I like lamb cooked medium-rare, but follow your own tastes. Lamb chops should be served right off the fire to ensure that the fat stays hot and crisp. Use small rib chops or the larger, meatier loin chops here. Lamb sirloin or lamb tenderloins would also work well. The Rosemary-Mint Paste is also delicious on rack of lamb and leg of lamb.

Make the herb paste: In a blender, food processor, or mortar, mash the herbs, garlic, salt, and pepper together, adding enough oil to make a thick paste.

Trim any excess fat from the lamb and rub the chops well on all sides with the herb paste. Wrap tightly in plastic wrap and refrigerate for up to 12 hours or let sit at room temperature for up to 1 hour. Bring the lamb to room temperature before cooking.

Make the Mint, Tomato, and Onion Relish: In a large bowl, combine the mint, tomatoes, and onions. In a small bowl, whisk the lemon juice, vinegar, and oil together and toss with the mint, tomatoes, and onions. Sprinkle with salt and pepper to taste.

Prepare the grill for direct cooking over medium-high heat (350°F). Brush or spray the grill with oil. Add hardwood chips or chunks following the directions on page 43.

Grill the lamb chops over direct heat for 3 to 5 minutes a side, depending on thickness and desired doneness. Move them to a cooler part of the grill if flare-ups occur. Lamb is medium-rare at 130°F to 135°F, firm to the touch, and pink at the center.

Serve the lamb chops with the Mint, Tomato, and Onion Relish and Vegetable Mixed Grill (page 181), with Pinot Noir from France's Burgundy region or New York's Long Island wine region.

New Mexican-Style Lamb Shoulder, Stuffed with Chiles and Garlic

SERVES 6 TO 8

4 New Mexican, Anaheim, poblano,
  or other green chiles
  (see Chiles, page 60)

1 (4-to-5-pound) boned lamb shoulder
  roast

Juice of 1 lemon

Salt

Ancho chile powder or blended chili
  powder, preferably Gebhardt

4 cloves garlic, minced

¼ cup chopped oregano or
  2 tablespoons dried

1 tablespoon ground cumin

Lamb shoulder has a rich, earthy flavor that combines beautifully with smoke and spices. Here I'm cooking it Southwest-Style with chiles, oregano, and cumin, but you could vary this recipe using other fresh herbs and spices. A stuffing of garlic, fresh parsley, chopped black olives, and dried tomatoes would give the lamb a southern French character or you could use the classic American stuffing of bread crumbs, onion, sage, and black pepper. It's best to buy lamb shoulder already boned by the butcher, as the primal cut has a good amount of bone and fat, which can be difficult to deal with. The boned roast already has the waste removed and can be untied and stuffed, then retied and roasted. Lamb shoulder is best roasted to medium-rare (135°F) or medium (140°F), since it has a higher fat content than leg of lamb or chops.

Prepare the grill for indirect cooking over medium-high heat (350°F), with a drip pan under the unheated portion of the grill. Add hardwood chips or chunks following the directions on page 43.

Grill the chiles over direct heat for 7 to 10 minutes, until charred and beginning to soften. Put into a sealed plastic or paper bag for 15 minutes. Scrape away the skin and remove the seeds and the stems. Cut into ½-inch-wide strips.

If tied, untie the boned roast, and trim and discard any excess fat or skin. Lay the lamb on a flat surface, cut side up. Rub both sides of the meat with the lemon juice and sprinkle all over with salt and chile powder. Put the chile strips down the middle of the cut side of the meat and sprinke with the garlic, oregano, and cumin. Roll and tie the roast in 4 or 5 places.

Place the roast on the unheated part of the grill over a drip pan and cook for 45 minutes to 1 hour, until medium rare or medium (135°F or 140°F for lamb). Begin checking the internal temperature with a meat thermometer after 30 minutes of cooking. Let the meat rest for 5 to 10 minutes.

Remove the strings and carve the roast. Serve with Three-Chile Salsa (page 75) and Campfire Beans (page 150).

Lamb Shoulder, Slow-Smoked Kentucky-Style

SERVES 6 TO 8

While pork is the barbecue meat of choice for most of the South, and Texans just love their smoky, long-cooked beef, folks in the border state of Kentucky are partial to mutton, slow-cooked in lots of smoke with sweet and spicy rubs, mops, and sauces. Mutton is hard to come by, in my neighborhood anyway, so I've used lamb shoulder for this Kentucky-style dish. I call for boned lamb shoulder, since I think it's the best value and easier to use, but you could also use a bone-in lamb shoulder roast here. I'd count on cooking plenty of lamb shoulder this way, since the shredded lamb heated in some sweet, hot barbecue sauce and served up on a sandwich bun with coleslaw on the side is one of the best 'cue sandwiches anyone ever dreamed of. The Sweet Hot Rub is also good on pork.

Sweet Hot Rub

2 tablespoons brown sugar

1 tablespoon hot Hungarian or Spanish paprika

1 tablespoon dried sage

1 tablespoon dried thyme

1 tablespoon black pepper

1 teaspoon cayenne, or more to taste

1 teaspoon ground allspice

½ tablespoon salt

1 (4-to-5-pound) boned lamb shoulder roast

Mint-Vinegar Mop

½ cup white vinegar

¼ cup Worcestershire sauce

1 cup tomato juice or beer

¼ cup chopped mint

1 teaspoon hot red pepper flakes, or more to taste

1 bunch mint for mopping (optional)

Barbecue sauce, homemade or storebought (optional)

Make the Sweet Hot Rub: In a small bowl, mix all the ingredients together. Sprinkle the mixture all over the lamb, wrap it tightly in plastic wrap, and refrigerate for up to 12 hours or let sit at room temperature for up to 2 hours. Bring the lamb to room temperature before cooking.

Make the Mint-Vinegar Mop: In a small bowl, mix all the ingredients together.

Prepare the grill for indirect cooking over low heat (275°F to 300°F), with a drip pan under the unheated portion of the grill. Add hardwood chips or chunks following the directions on page 43.

Put the lamb over the drip pan on the unheated portion of the grill and cook at low heat with plenty of wood smoke for 2 to 3 hours, until the meat is very tender and the interior temperature reaches 165°F. Use a bunch of fresh mint, a clean dish mop, or a brush to apply the mop to the meat during cooking, starting after the first 30 minutes and mopping the meat often as it cooks.

Serve the meat shredded or carved into chunks, with barbecue sauce, if you wish, and Grilled Corn with Garlic-Chile Butter (see page 191).

Vegetables & Fruit

When I remember how my mother cooked summer squash, cutting zucchini into chunks and boiling it for what seemed hours until it was a stringy mush, I wonder that I ever ate it again. I certainly did my best to avoid squash as a kid, artfully (but usually unsuccessfully) hiding it under the mashed potatoes. Then I tasted zucchini that had been marinated briefly in oil and basil and garlic, then grilled for a minute or two over a smoky fire, and I had a revelation, a kind of squash conversion. This was good. Even more: This once-scorned vegetable was absolutely delicious hot off the grill.

From then on my love affair with grilled vegetables continued. Why boil any vegetable ever again, I asked myself? So I grilled corn, and asparagus, and green beans, and eggplants, and tomatoes—just about anything I could grow in my garden I could cook on the grill, I thought.

TACOS AND BURRITOS

Tacos and burritos are constant fare at my house. They are one of the reasons I advocate cooking more than you can eat every time you grill (see Leftovers, page 84). If I arrive home harried and rushed, I'm likely to open up the refrigerator, take out a bottle of that good Mexican ale, Bohemia, and whatever I else find on the shelves, and put together some tacos or burritos, depending on what type of tortillas I have at the time: corn for tacos, flour for burritos.

I almost always have some homemade salsa around, but if not, it's only a few minutes' work to grill some tomatoes and an onion or two, soak a dried chile in warm water or chop up a fresh one, and toss them into the blender to make a quick puree. I add a squeeze or two of lime or lemon, a bit of salt, and maybe some Tapatio or other hot sauce, and my salsa is made. And then I chop up the grilled chicken or grilled swordfish or grilled pork tenderloin or grilled zucchini that I found, tuck it into a quick-grilled tortilla with some salsa and chopped lettuce or cooked beans, and I've made myself and my wife some really tasty tacos or burritos. Quick, easy, and delicious.

Well, I haven't grilled lettuce, although I have grilled radicchio and bok choy and chard stems. And I've not yet figured out how to grill carrots, but beets are fantastic when wrapped in foil with a bit of butter and lemon and roasted over indirect heat. Potatoes? No problem: Bake them, or parboil larger new potatoes and grill them, or just put tiny new potatoes over the coals. Peppers? Toss them right onto high heat to char and soften, put them in a bag to steam, scrape off the skin, and dig in.

And now I'm grilling fruits of all kinds too. Peaches and pears and bananas, cut in half, dipped in lemon juice and brown sugar, and grilled directly over medium-high heat—the perfect dessert on a summer evening with a scoop of ice cream or a berry-flavored yogurt or cream. Grilled pineapple is wonderful by itself, or with a fragrant sauce of rum and vanilla, or cut into chunks and added to a spicy salsa.

My daughter Meghan has become an expert baker in her small kettle grill, making berry and fruit cobblers and crisps and cooking them over indirect heat. She is now the dessert maker whenever she comes to dinner. After I've served the main course hot from the grill, she puts on her berry cobbler or peach crisp to cook in the remaining heat while we sit down at the table. By the time we've finished, the dessert is brown and bubbly and ready to eat.

Eggplant Grilled in Oregano Smoke

SERVES 6 TO 8 AS A SIDE DISH, 4 AS A MAIN COURSE

4 globe eggplants or 8 Japanese
  eggplants

Garlic and Oregano Marinade

2 cups olive oil

Juice of 2 lemons

6 cloves garlic, minced

¼ cup chopped oregano or
  2 tablespoons dried

1 teaspoon salt

1 teaspoon black pepper

Oregano branches

When I taught wine classes and I would describe a rich, complex red Bordeaux or a big, brawny Zinfandel from California's foothills, invariably somebody would ask me what food would go with the wine. I'd suggest grilled porterhouse or butterflied leg of lamb, and, being in Berkeley, I'd usually hear a voice from the back of the room exclaiming, "But I'm a vegetarian!" My answer was always, "Eggplant! The wine goes beautifully with eggplant." Well, I might have been winging it a bit, but eggplant is so rich and meaty that it does go well with most red wines and can be the centerpiece of a hearty vegetarian feast. Grilling eggplant brings out the meaty character of the vegetable and cuts down on the amount of oil that eggplant seems to soak up when it's sauteed. Leftover grilled eggplant is excellent chopped, with grilled tomatoes (see page 103), over pasta, or on sandwiches, or mashed with roasted garlic (see page 159) for a wonderful topping for bruschetta (see page 93). Burning soaked herbs in the fire adds a lovely smoky aroma to the food. I use oregano, but any woody herb will do.

Cut the eggplants into ½-inch-thick slices: globe eggplants into rounds, Japanese or other Asian eggplants lengthwise. Combine all the marinade ingredients and put the eggplant in a flat dish with the marinade, turning once or twice to coat both sides of the slices. Let sit at room temperature for up to 1 hour, turning once or twice.

Prepare the grill for direct cooking over high heat (375°F to 400°F). Soak the oregano branches for at least 30 minutes before you begin grilling.

Add the oregano branches to the fire, following the directions on page 44. Grill the eggplant slices over direct heat for 3 to 5 minutes per side until nicely browned and beginning to soften. Brush with the marinade a few times during cooking. Move the eggplant pieces to a cooler part of the grill if flare-ups occur. Do not overcook.

Brush the eggplant slices with any remaining marinade after you remove them from the grill. Serve as a side dish, a main course with a salad and garlic bread, or on split rolls as sandwiches—with a full-bodied red wine, of course.

Grilled Summer Squash with Fresh Herb Marinade

SERVES 6 TO 8 AS A SIDE DISH, 4 AS A MAIN DISH

When the garden goes into full production and the zucchini begin to seem like an endlessly proliferating alien species, this is the time to get the grill hot and toss on any kind of summer squash you have plenty of—zukes, pattypan, crookneck, or whatever else is flourishing. Grilling squash is easy and quick and is infinitely superior to boiling or steaming or stewing these delicate vegetables. Grilling sears the outside and keeps juices in. And on the grill you're not likely to overcook squash the way Mom used to do when that watery mess on the plate was called "squash, and you'd better eat every bit of it!" Cooking times will vary with the size and thickness of the squash and how you slice them. The rule: Less is better! I like to put slices of summer squash in a tasty marinade while I cook the other dishes, and then just sear the squash on the grill over the highest heat I can find. A few minutes is all you need. Serve as a side dish or main course or chopped, with grilled tomatoes (see page 103), over pasta.

12 medium summer squash, such as zucchini, pattypan or crookneck

Fresh Herb Marinade

2 cups olive oil

¼ cup balsamic vinegar

Juice of 1 lemon

4 cloves garlic, minced

¼ cup chopped basil or 2 tablespoons dried

¼ cup chopped oregano or 2 tablespoons dried

1 teaspoon salt

1 teaspoon black pepper

Salt and pepper

Slice the squash into ¾-inch-thick pieces. Combine all the marinade ingredients and put the squash slices in a flat dish with the marinade, turning the squash once or twice to coat both sides. Let sit for up to 1 hour before cooking. Remove from the marinade and pat the squash pieces dry before cooking.

Prepare the grill for direct cooking over high heat (375°F to 400°F).

Grill the squash slices over high heat for 2 to 4 minutes per side, until grill-marked and beginning to soften. Do not overcook. Brush with any remaining marinade and sprinkle with salt and pepper, then serve.

Vegetable Mixed Grill

SERVES 4

Just about any vegetable you can grow in your garden, you can cook on the grill. Go on the assumption that if you can eat a vegetable raw, then a couple of minutes on the grill will heat it and sear the outside to keep juices in. Add flavor using an oil with herbs or garlic or a simple vinaigrette, and you've got a delicious side dish or addition to a salad, pasta, or soup. In this recipe I grill eggplant, summer squash, peppers, and onion, but you could use any combination that suits your fancy. The secret to grilling vegetables: Get the grill good and hot, use an oil flavored with garlic and/or herbs to annoint the vegetables before, during, and after grilling, and keep it quick.

1 globe eggplant

4 to 6 zucchini

4 to 6 pattypan or crookneck squash

1 large red onion

1 red bell pepper

1 yellow bell pepper

Basil Garlic Oil (page 86) or other flavored oils (page 162)

Grilled Tomato Sauce with Basil and Garlic (page 183) or other tomato sauce, warmed

Prepare the grill for direct cooking over high heat (375°F to 400°F).

Slice the eggplant into ½-inch rounds. Cut the zucchini lengthwise into ½-inch slices. Cut the pattypan or crookneck squash into ½-inch-thick slices. Cut the onion into ½-inch slices. Leave the bell peppers whole.

Grill the peppers over direct heat for 7 to 10 minutes, turning often to char the skin on all sides, then put them in a sealed plastic or paper bag to steam for 15 minutes. Scrape off the skin, discard the stems and seeds, and either slice into thick strips or chop coarsely.

Brush all sides of all the vegetables with the flavored oil and cook the eggplant, zucchini, and squash over direct heat for 3 to 5 minutes per side, turning once or twice, until grill-marked and starting to soften. You may brush the vegetables with flavored oil during cooking, if you wish. If flare-ups occur, move the vegetables to a cooler part of the grill.

At this point you can make your choice: Either arrange the vegetables in large pieces on a colorful platter and spoon the warm tomato sauce over them to serve as a vegetarian main course or as a side dish. Or you can chop all the vegetables coarsely and mix them with the warm tomato sauce to serve over pasta for a main course or as a side dish.

Grilled Tomatoes Three Ways

Grilling tomatoes in woodsmoke before using them in a sauce results in a wonderfully sweet and smoky taste that seems to accentuate the sauce's flavor. It's simple: Just rub whole tomatoes with a little olive oil and put them over direct heat in the smokiest part of the grill. A few minutes is all you need, turning the tomatoes from time to time, until grill-marked. Take them off if they are splitting or starting to sag on the grill. If I'm cooking a roast or a bird by indirect heat, I'll often pass the time by grilling a batch of tomatoes. I let them cool, then pack the tomatoes in resealable plastic bags, and put them in the fridge or freezer for later use. This is a good way to use up the summer's bounty from the garden or farmer's markets.

Grilled Tomato Sauce with Red Peppers and Tarragon

Use this sauce with grilled fish or poultry, on pasta, or wherever you want the taste of tomatoes and tarragon.

Olive oil
6 to 8 medium tomatoes
1 onion, cut into ½-inch rounds
1 red bell pepper
2 cloves garlic, minced, or 4 cloves roast garlic (see page 159)
¼ cup chopped fresh tarragon or 2 tablespoons dried
2 tablespoons tarragon or sherry vinegar
½ teaspoon cayenne
1 teaspoon salt
½ teaspoon black pepper

Prepare the grill for direct cooking over medium-high heat (350°F). Add hardwood chips or chunks following the directions on page 43.

Rub the tomatoes with oil and grill over high heat, turning often, for 6 to 8 minutes, until grill-marked and beginning to soften. Remove the tomatoes from the grill if the skin breaks or if they begin to sag or char. Do not overcook. Brush the onion rounds with oil and grill for 3 to 5 minutes per side, until grill-marked and beginning to soften. Grill the pepper over direct heat for 7 to 10 minutes, turning often, until the skin is charred. Put it in a sealed plastic or paper bag to steam for 15 minutes. Scrape off the peel and discard the seeds and stem. Either coarsely chop the tomatoes, onions, and bell pepper by hand or process them in a food processor or blender to a coarse puree. Blend with the remaining ingredients.

Grilled Tomato Sauce with Chiles, Onion, and Lime

Use with tacos, burritos, enchiladas, or wherever you want a Southwestern flavor.

Olive oil

6 to 8 tomatoes

1 onion, cut into ½-inch rounds

1 large green chile such as Anaheim or New Mexico (see Chiles, page 60)

1 dried chile such as ancho or pasilla, soaked for 30 minutes in hot water to cover (optional)

1 jalapeño or serrano chile, stemmed, seeded, and finely chopped

¼ cup chopped fresh oregano or 2 tablespoons dried

2 cloves garlic, minced or 4 cloves roast garlic (see page 159)

Juice of 2 limes

1 teaspoon salt

Prepare the grill for direct cooking over medium-high heat (350°F). Add hardwood chips or chunks following the directions on page 43.

Rub the tomatoes with oil and grill over high heat, turning often, for 6 to 8 minutes, until grill-marked and beginning to soften. Remove the tomatoes from the grill if the skin breaks or if they begin to sag or char. Do not overcook. Brush the onion rounds with oil and grill for 3 to 5 minutes per side, until grill-marked and beginning to soften. Grill the green chile over direct heat for about 10 minutes, turning often, until the skin is charred. Put the chile in a sealed plastic or paper bag to soften for 15 minutes. Scrape off the peel and discard the seeds and stem.

If using the dried chile, remove it from the soaking water, remove the stem and the seeds, tear it up into pieces, and add to a blender or food processor with a little of the soaking liquid. Process to a thin paste.

Either coarsely chop the tomatoes, onions, and green chile by hand or process them in a food processor or blender to a coarse puree. Combine with the chile paste and the remaining ingredients.

Grilled Tomato Sauce with Basil and Garlic

Use on pasta, pizza, bruschetta, or in any recipe that calls for Italian-style tomato sauce.

Olive oil

6 to 8 medium tomatoes

3 cloves garlic, minced, or 6 cloves roast garlic (see page 159)

¼ cup chopped fresh basil or 2 tablespoons dried

2 tablespoons extra-virgin olive oil

1 teaspoon salt

½ teaspoon black pepper

½ teaspoon red pepper flakes, or more to taste

Prepare the grill for cooking over medium-high heat (350°F). Add hardwood chips or chunks following the directions on page 43.

Rub the tomatoes with oil and grill over high heat, turning often, for 6 to 8 minutes, until grill-marked and beginning to soften. Remove the tomatoes from the grill if the skin breaks or if they begin to sag or char. Do not overcook.

Let the tomatoes cool slightly and either chop them by hand or process them in a blender or food processor to a coarse puree. Stir in the remaining ingredients and serve at room temperature or warmed through in a microwave oven or on the stove.

Basic Pizza Crust

MAKES 2 (10-INCH) PIZZA CRUSTS

1 package (¼ ounce) active dry yeast

1 teaspoon sugar

2 cups all-purpose flour, plus more as needed to prevent sticking

½ teaspoon salt

1 tablespoon dried herbs (basil, oregano, rosemary, thyme, optional

¼ cup olive oil, plus more for brushing

1 tablespoon cornmeal

You can use this basic dough recipe to create any of your own favorite pizzas or follow the recipes here. Add whatever toppings you like, from spicy to sweet. I like to add dried herbs such as basil, oregano, rosemary, and/or thyme to my savory doughs, and spices and aromatics like cinnamon, nutmeg, Chinese five-spice powder and/or vanilla and almond extract or ginger juice to doughs for fruit and other sweet toppings.

Combine the yeast, sugar, and ¾ cup warm water. Let the mixture stand in a warm place for at least 5 minutes, or until bubbles form.

In a separate bowl, combine 2 cups of the flour with the salt and herbs. Make a well in the dry ingredients. Add the yeast mixture and ¼ cup of the oil to the center of the dry ingredients. Mix with your fingers, gradually incorporating the dry ingredients into the wet, until the dough forms a ball. If the dough seems too sticky, add more flour.

On a lightly floured surface, knead the dough for 10 minutes. You can also use a food processor with a dough hook on high speed for about 8 minutes.

Form the dough into a ball and dust with flour. Coat a large bowl with oil, place the dough in it, and cover with plastic wrap or a lid. Put the bowl in a warm place for 1 to 2 hours, or until the dough has doubled in size.

Punch down the dough with your fist. Divide it into 2 equal pieces. On a lightly floured surface, knead each piece for about 4 minutes. (At this point, if you'd like, you can wrap the pieces in plastic wrap and store them in the refrigerator for up to 1 week, or you can freeze them.)

Prepare the grill for indirect cooking at very high heat (400°F to 450°F). Brush or spray the grill with oil.

Stretch each ball out a bit and then roll from the center outward to form a 10-inch circle about ¼ inch thick. If you are using a gas grill where the burners are close together, you might have to make an oblong or a rectangle to fit the unheated portion

PIZZA ON THE GRILL

Baking pizza on the grill is easier than it sounds. A kettle grill or covered gas grill is all you need, since both function as outdoor ovens when the cover is down and you are cooking by indirect heat. A built-in thermometer helps keep track of temperatures, but an old-fashioned oven thermometer placed on the unheated portion of the grill will do almost as well. You can use the Basic Pizza Crust, opposite, or your favorite pizza dough recipe, or simply buy one of the prebaked pizza rounds at the market and put on any of the topping combinations in the recipes that follow, or your own favorite toppings. While most pizzas are of the savory variety, you can also make delicious fruit or other dessert pizzas (page 189) if you change the dough recipe as described in the variation (below).

of the grill. If holes appear, fold the dough over on itself to seal them. Crimp the edge to form a rim. Brush the top of the dough with oil and sprinkle half of the cornmeal on it.

Place the dough, oiled side down, on the unheated part of the grill, and cook for 3 to 5 minutes. While it is grilling, brush the other side with oil and sprinkle with the rest of the cornmeal. Using a metal spatula, carefully flip the dough, trying not to tear the crust. Grill the other side for 3 to 5 minutes, or until both sides are firm to the touch and beginning to brown.

Remove the crust from the grill. Proceed with any of the pizza recipes that follow.

Variation: For a sweet dessert pizza crust, instead of the herbs use 1 tablespoon dried spices (ginger, cinnamon, nutmeg, and/or Chinese five-spice powder), and when you pour the liquid ingredients into the dry, you can also add 1 teaspoon vanilla extract, almond extract, and/or ginger juice. Make the crimped edge extra-high to accommodate the juiciness of fruit toppings. Instead of oil, brush the dough with 2 tablespoons melted butter. Omit the cornmeal.

Classic Cheese Pizza

MAKES 2 (10-INCH) PIZZAS; SERVES 4

1 red onion, cut into ½-inch rounds

1 Basic Pizza Crust (page 184) or
   two 10- inch precooked pizza crusts

2 cups Grilled Tomato Sauce with
   Basil and Garlic (page 183),
   or homemade or store-bought
   tomato sauce

1 cup cherry tomatoes, stems
   removed, halved

½ cup chopped fresh basil

2 cloves garlic, finely chopped

1 cup grated mozzarella cheese

1 teaspoon salt

½ teaspoon black pepper

Olive oil

To make this pizza or any other on the grill, use the recipe for pizza dough (page 184) or your own favorite homemade dough recipe or a premade crust. This is America's classic pizza with tomato sauce and mozzarella cheese. Add your own favorite toppings as you wish: sliced mushrooms, slices of pepperoni or precooked sausage, roasted and peeled green, red, or yellow bell peppers, pitted black olives, raw or grilled onions, and so on. You can hold or not hold the anchovies and add extra cheese or garlic or whatever else you have a yen for.

Prepare the grill for indirect cooking over very high heat (400°F to 450°F). Brush or spray the grill with oil.

Grill the onion slices over direct heat for 2 to 3 minutes per side, until grill-marked and starting to soften. Remove from the grill and chop coarsely.

Follow the directions for preparing and cooking Basic Pizza Crust (page 184). If you are using prebaked pizza crusts, grill them over indirect heat for 2 to 3 minutes per side to heat through, or follow the package directions for heating.

Remove the crusts from the grill, divide the toppings between the 2 crusts, and layer on the tomato sauce, chopped onion, cherry tomatoes, basil, and garlic. Spread the cheese over the vegetables and sprinkle with the salt, pepper, and oil. Bake the pizzas on the unheated part of the grill, covered, for 5 to 10 minutes, or until the cheese has melted and is beginning to brown. Serve immediately.

Roast Garlic and Chicken Pizza

MAKES 2 (10-INCH) PIZZAS; SERVES 4

Pizza is a great way to use up leftover roast or grilled chicken. Here we combine chicken with roast garlic and olives, but you could also use leftover grilled chiles or bell peppers, any grilled vegetables, grilled seafood or fish, or whatever takes your fancy.

1 head of garlic

Olive oil

1 recipe Basic Pizza Crust (page 184), or 2 (10-inch) precooked pizza crusts

2 cups chopped grilled tomatoes (see page 103) or chopped fresh or canned tomatoes

2 grilled chicken breasts, chopped, or 3 to 4 cups chopped cooked chicken

½ cup chopped pitted black olives

¼ cup chopped fresh oregano or 2 tablespoons dried

1 teaspoon salt

½ teaspoon black pepper

Basil Garlic Oil (page 86) or other flavored oil (page 162)

Prepare the grill for indirect cooking over very high heat (400°F to 450°F). Brush or spray the grill with oil.

To roast the garlic, slice off about ¼ inch from the top or stem of the garlic head, exposing the tops of the cloves. Rub the head of garlic with olive oil and wrap it in oiled heavy-duty foil. Place the foil-wrapped garlic on the unheated part of the grill or on a roasting rack and cook for 30 to 40 minutes, until the cloves are soft.

Follow the directions for preparing and cooking Basic Pizza Crust (page 184). If you are using prebaked pizza crusts, grill them over indirect heat for 2 to 3 minutes per side to heat through, or follow the package directions for heating.

Remove the crusts from the grill and, dividing the toppings between the 2 crusts, layer on the tomatoes, chicken, and olives. Remove the cloves from the head of garlic and divide them between the pizzas. Sprinkle with the oregano, salt, pepper, and flavored oil. Bake the pizzas on the unheated part of the grill, covered, for 5 to 10 minutes, or until the chicken and garlic are beginning to brown. Serve immediately.

Chèvre, Zucchini, Eggplant, and Roasted Pepper Pizza

MAKES 2 (10-INCH) PIZZAS; SERVES 4

1 recipe Basic Pizza Crust (page 184), or 2 (10- inch) precooked pizza crusts

1 zucchini, cut lengthwise into ½-inch-thick slices

1 globe eggplant, sliced into ½-inch rounds

3 tomatoes

1 red bell pepper

2 cloves garlic, finely chopped

Olive oil

¼ cup chopped basil

1 cup fresh chèvre or other goat cheese, crumbled

1 teaspoon salt

½ teaspoon black pepper

Basil Garlic Oil (page 86) or other flavored oil

This recipe works well with leftover Vegetable Mixed Grill (page 181), Grilled Summer Squash with Fresh Herb Marinade (page 179), Eggplant Grilled in Oregano Smoke (page 179), Grilled Chile Rajas (page 119), or virtually any grilled vegetable from your garden or the farmer's market. Experiment with different types of grilled vegetables. Try adding different fresh or dried herbs to your pizza dough for added flavor.

Prepare the grill for indirect cooking over very high heat (400°F to 450°F). Brush or spray the grill with oil.

Brush the zucchini, eggplant, tomatoes, and bell peppers with olive oil. Over direct heat, grill the zucchini and eggplant slices for 5 to 7 minutes, turning often, until grill-marked and beginning to soften. Grill the tomatoes over direct heat for 5 to 7 minutes turning often. Grill and char the bell pepper for 7 to 10 minutes, turning often. Place the pepper in a sealed plastic or paper bag to steam for 15 minutes. Scrape off most of the skin and discard the stem and seeds. Coarsely chop the zucchini, eggplant, tomatoes, and pepper and combine them with the garlic.

Follow the directions for preparing and cooking Basic Pizza Crust (page 184). If you are using precooked pizza crusts, grill them over indirect heat for 2 to 3 minutes per side to heat through, or follow the package directions for heating.

Remove the crusts from the grill and, dividing the toppings between the 2 crusts, layer the chopped vegetables on top. Spread the chèvre over the vegetables and sprinkle with the salt, pepper, and flavored oil. Bake the pizzas on the unheated part of the grill, covered, for 5 minutes, or until the cheese has melted and is beginning to brown. Serve immediately.

Grilled Fruit Pizza

Yes, you read it right. You can make delicious dessert pizzas on the grill using grilled fruit, raw berries, cherries, or even cooked, sweetened rhubarb, if it pleases you. The trick is to make a dough with sweet spice, as directed in the basic crust recipe, and then layer on whatever fruit you want. Grill pears, peaches, apples, pineapples, or other hard fruit (see page 193), or use strawberries, blueberries, raspberries, kiwi, or other soft fruit raw. Combine fruits as you desire. I use grilled pears in this recipe, but virtually any fruit will do.

6 cups chopped or sliced grilled pears or other fruit (see page 193)

1 tablespoon lemon juice

½ cup firmly packed light brown sugar

1 recipe Basic Pizza Crust, sweet variation (page 184–85), or 2 (10-inch) precooked pizza crusts

2 tablespoons cold butter, chopped

In a large bowl, toss the fruit with the lemon juice and brown sugar.

Prepare the grill for indirect cooking over very high heat (400°F to 450°F). Brush or spray the grill with oil.

Follow the directions for preparing and cooking Basic Pizza Crust (page 184). If using precooked pizza crusts, grill them over indirect heat for 2 to 3 minutes per side to heat through, or follow the package directions for heating.

Remove the crusts from the grill and divide the fruit topping between the 2 crusts. Dot with pieces of cold butter. Bake the pizzas on the grill, covered, over indirect heat for 5 minutes, or until the fruit is heated through and is beginning to brown. Serve immediately.

Grilled Portobello Mushrooms

SERVES 6 TO 8 AS A SIDE DISH OR ON SANDWICHES, 4 AS A MAIN COURSE

8 portobello mushroom caps

¼ cup Garlic and Basil Oil (page 86), or other flavored oil (page 162)

Salt and pepper

Portobello mushrooms are large brown mushrooms that have a meaty, earthy flavor that is accentuated by quick grilling in aromatic wood smoke. You can serve grilled portobellos sliced as a garnish for steak or grilled chicken or whole as a centerpiece for a vegetarian feast or to replace meat patties in a tasty mushroom burger. Use the large caps for grilling, and save the stems for Sherry Mushroom Gravy (page 144) or to use in soups, sauces, or on pasta. Smaller mushrooms can be skewered and used in this recipe.

Prepare the grill for direct cooking over medium-high heat (350°F).

Clean the mushrooms by brushing or rinsing briefly in cold water and patting dry. Brush both sides of the caps with the flavored oil and sprinkle liberally with salt and pepper.

Put all the mushrooms, gill side up, over direct heat and grill for 2 to 3 minutes. Turn, dumping out any liquid that has accumulated in the caps into the fire. Brush with more oil. Grill for another 2 to 3 minutes, turn the mushrooms, and brush again with the oil. Grill for another minute, or until grill-marked and beginning to soften. Do not overcook.

Serve the mushrooms, sliced and sprinkled with flavored oil, as a side dish for grilled meat or poultry. Or make a sandwich by putting one or two caps in a split, toasted roll and drizzling with more oil. You can also serve whole grilled mushrooms with Smoked Tomato Risotto (page 96) for an elegant vegetarian main course.

Grilled Corn with Chile-Garlic Butter

SERVES 4 TO 6

Fresh corn hot of the grill is a tasty summer treat. Grilling seals in flavors and adds a little crunch and smoke to the tender kernels of just-picked corn. Get the freshest corn you can find, from your garden, a farmer's market, or a roadside stand, and get it on the grill as quick as you can. Some folks swear by soaking corn first and grilling it in the husks, but I like to shuck the corn, rub it with a flavored butter, and put it right on the heat. You'll find directions for both techniques below. I often grill corn and other vegetables over direct heat while I'm cooking whole chickens or a roast on indirect heat. Grill plenty of vegetables, as they all go well on pizzas or in pasta dishes, in salsas or sauces. Flavored butters like the Chile-Garlic Butter below are delicious on grilled vegetables, but are also very tasty with grilled fish or seafood or grilled meats of any type. Vary the herbs and spices in flavored butters as your taste buds dictate.

Chile-Garlic Butter

- 1 dried chile such as ancho, pasilla (see Chiles, page 60), or ¼ cup blended chili powder, preferably Gebhardt
- 2 cloves garlic, minced, or 4 cloves roast garlic (see page 159)
- ½ pound salted butter, softened
- Salt and pepper to taste

- 8 ears fresh corn, unhusked or husked

Prepare the grill for direct cooking over medium-high heat (350°F). Brush or spray the grill with oil.

Make the Chile-Garlic Butter: Soak the dried chile in hot water to cover 30 minutes, then remove from the water and discard the stem and seeds. Put into a blender or food processor with a little of the soaking water and process to a coarse paste. With a fork or a potato masher, mix the chile paste or chili powder with the garlic and softened butter.

Husk the corn or not, depending on your preference. If cooking husked corn, brush the corn before cooking and 3 or 4 times during cooking with the Chile-Garlic Butter. Grill the husked or unhusked ears over direct heat, turning often, until grill-marked and heated through, about 10 minutes total. A little char on the corn adds to the flavor, but do not overcook. If cooking corn with the husks still on, remove the corn from the fire when done, husk, and brush with the Chile-Garlic Butter. Sprinkle the corn with salt and pepper.

Serve the corn hot off the grill slathered with Chile-Garlic Butter.

Grilled Peaches with Berry Coulis

Grilling fruit creates a caramelized crust and warms the sweet juices to provide a delectable dessert when paired with ice cream, sorbet, or a light and flavorful sauce like this one based on fresh berries. I use peaches in this recipe, but nectarines, pears, pineapple, banana, or other fruit can be easily substituted. When choosing fruit, it's best to pick fruit that is not quite fully ripe so that it doesn't fall apart on the grill. Use a grill basket or perforated grid if it looks like the fruit might fall through the grill. Do not overcook: The fruit should be lightly browned and just warmed through. Delicious fruit and berry syrups are made by Torani, an Italian producer, or by domestic jam makers such as Knott's Berry Farm or Smucker's. Use a fruit- or berry-flavored liqueur or brandy or an eau de vie from Alsace, California, or Oregon in the coulis.

4 peaches, halved and pitted

Lemon juice

½ cup brown sugar

Berry Coulis

2 cups fresh or frozen berries (blackberries, blueberries, etc.)

2 tablespoons berry syrup, or more to taste

1 ounce berry liqueur or brandy

Prepare the grill for direct cooking over high heat (375°F to 400°F). Clean the grill well and brush or spray with oil.

Rub the cut side of each peach half with lemon juice and dip into brown sugar on a plate to coat thoroughly. Grill, cut side down, over direct heat for 3 to 5 minutes, or until grill-marked and lightly browned. Turn and grill for another 3 to 5 minutes until warmed through. Remove from the grill.

Make the Berry Coulis: Mash 1 cup of the berries together with the syrup and liqueur.

Spoon the coulis over the peaches and garnish with the remaining whole berries.

Raspberry Apple Crisp

SERVES 6 TO 8

8 cups cored, sliced apples (about 5 to 6
    medium apples)
Juice of 1 lemon
½ cup packed brown sugar
¼ teaspoon Chinese five-spice powder
1½ cups raspberries

Five-Spice Crisp Topping
¾ cup all-purpose flour
¾ cup brown sugar
½ teaspoon Chinese five-spice powder
½ teaspoon cinnamon
8 tablespoons (1 stick) cold butter

Baking crisps and cobblers on the grill is a fine way to enjoy the abundant harvest of summer fruits and berries. I use apples and raspberries in this recipe, but you can vary it with fruits in season. The crisp topping below incorporates Chinese five-spice powder, an unusual but intriguing flavor. You could also season the crisp topping or your favorite cobbler or biscuit dough with vanilla, allspice, nutmeg, dried ginger, and/or other spices and aromatics. The easiest and most convenient baking pans for the grill are the 9-by-13-inch foil pans sold by grill manufacturers as drip pans.

Prepare the grill for indirect cooking over medium-high heat (375°F to 400°F).

In a large bowl, combine the apples, lemon juice, ½ cup brown sugar, and ¼ teaspoon Chinese five-spice powder. Mix until apples are well coated. Put the apple mixture in an ungreased 9-by-13-inch ovenproof pan. Sprinkle the raspberries on top of the apples.

Make the Five-Spice Crisp Topping: In a large bowl, combine the flour, brown sugar, five-spice powder, and cinnamon. Add the butter in small chunks and cut it in with a fork, a pastry cutter, or your fingers until the mixture resembles coarse bread crumbs.

Spread the crisp topping in a layer on top of the fruit. Tap the pan on the counter to distribute the fruit evenly. Place on the unheated portion of the grill and bake, covered, for 1 hour or until the topping has browned and the apples are tender when pierced with a skewer or fork.

Serve the crisp warm, with vanilla ice cream or vary the Berry Cream recipe (page 195) with raspberries and raspberry syrup.

Skewered Strawberries and Bananas with Berry Cream

SERVES 4

Pick big strawberries and large, firm bananas for this delicious and dramatic dessert. I find that using two small wood skewers stabilizes the fruits better, but try whatever skewers work best for you. You can also skewer and grill other fruits: chunks of pineapple; thick slices of peach, nectarine, or pear; halved kiwis or small papayas. The Berry Cream is quick and easy, and can be made with any kind of berry or soft fruit. Torani, an Italian producer of syrups for ices and drinks, makes a wide variety of flavored syrups that are available in Italian delicatessens and by mail order (see Sources, page 200).

12 large strawberries,
  stems removed

2 to 3 bananas, cut into
  2-inch pieces

Juice of 1 lemon

¾ cup packed brown sugar

Berry Cream

1 cup heavy cream

¼ cup chopped or mashed
  strawberries or other berries

2 tablespoons strawberry or
  other flavored syrup

Sugar to taste

Prepare the grill for direct cooking over high heat (375°F to 400°F). Clean the grill well and brush or spray with oil. Soak wood skewers, if you are using them, for 30 minutes before grilling.

In a large bowl, toss the fruit in the lemon juice and sprinkle with the brown sugar. Skewer the strawberries and bananas alternately on wood or metal skewers. Use 2 parallel skewers to stabilize the fruit, if you wish.

Grill the fruit over direct heat for 3 to 5 minutes on each side, until lightly browned and beginning to soften. Do not overcook. Handle the skewers carefully and remove them from the fire if the fruit starts to fall off. Use a grill basket or perforated grid if it looks like the fruit will fall through the grill.

Make the Berry Cream: Put the cream, berries, and syrup in an electric mixer and whip until soft peaks form. Add sugar to taste.

Spoon the cream over the warm fruit and serve immediately.

Grilled Pineapple with Rum and Ginger Sauce

SERVES 4

8 (½-inch-thick) slices fresh
  pineapple

½ cup dark rum

½ cup packed brown sugar

Rum and Ginger Sauce

½ cup brown sugar

½ cup reserved rum

Juice of 1 lime

1 tablespoon cornstarch

¼ cup pineapple juice

¼ cup chopped candied ginger (optional)

Whipped cream and mint for garnish
  (optional)

Pineapple is one of my favorite fruits on the grill. The natural sweetness of the fruit is accentuated, and the caramelized surface adds even more flavor. Serve grilled pineapple as a dessert with a sweet sauce, as here, or in a tangy salsa or relish (page 91). Use a whole pineapple or precut slices from the market.

Prepare the grill for direct cooking over high heat (375°F to 400°F). Clean the grill well and brush or spray with oil.

Soak the pineapple slices in the rum for at least 30 minutes, turning once or twice. Reserved the rum and any juices for the Rum and Ginger Sauce.

Dip the pineapple slices into brown sugar on a flat plate to coat both sides thoroughly. Grill over direct heat for 3 to 5 minutes per side, until grill-marked and lightly browned.

Make the sauce: In a nonreactive saucepan over medium-low heat, stir together the brown sugar, the reserved rum and juices, and the lime juice. Be careful not to ignite the rum. Mix the cornstarch with the pineapple juice, whisk the mixture into the saucepan, and simmer for 5 to 6 minutes until the sauce thickens. Stir in the (optional) candied ginger.

Spoon the warm sauce over the pineapple slices, with a dollop of whipped cream and a mint leaf if you like.

tenderloin marinated in rum and ginger with grilled pineapple–onion relish, 117
tenderloin with chipotle rub and grilled chiles and onions, 112–13
tenderloin with sage and black pepper rub and garlic-chile grits, 114–16, *115*
see also Bacon; Rib(s)
Portobello mushrooms, grilled, 190
Potato(es), 176
    new, smoke-roasted, *148, 149,* 151
    salad, Jan's seaside, 155
    smoke-baked, 151
Poultry, 83–107
    duck, roast, with ginger-honey glaze, *104, 105*
    duck breast, peppery, with Creole gravy, 102–3
    game hens, Southwest, under a brick with tomatillo-jícama salad, 99
    quail or game hens, bacon-wrapped, campfire style, *100, 101*
    turkey, roast, with herb and pepper rub and smoke-roasted yams, 107
    turkey or chicken thighs, chipotle, 106
    see also Chicken
Prawns, 64
    Gulf Coast, with lemon and sweet pepper relish, *66, 67*

Q

Quail, bacon-wrapped, campfire style, *100, 101*

R

Rajas, grilled chile, 119
Raspberry apple crisp, 194
Red wine marinade, 165
Relishes:
    corn, grilled, chow-chow, 72
    lemon and sweet pepper, *66, 67*
    mint, tomato, and onion, 170, *171*
    pineapple, grilled, and onion, 117
    pineapple-chile chutney, 133
Rib(s), 110
    baby back, chile-ginger, with plum sauce glaze, 124
    baby back, peppery, with smoky tomato barbecue sauce, 125
    country, smoke-roasted, with vinegar-chile mop and hot greens, 133
    country-style, Chinatown, with hoisin-mustard glaze, 122
    cuts of, 127
    rubs, Jeff's, 125, 126
    short, cow-country Dutch oven, 158, *159*
    spareribs, slow-cooked, two ways, 126–27
Rice:
    adobo, 166
    dirty, 120
    smoked tomato risotto, 96–97
    sweet and sour, 69
Risotto, smoked tomato, 96–97
Roasting, 13–14, 34
    grilling combined with, 34, 36–37
    indirect, 37
    slow-, *37–38*

Rosemary, 44–45
    mint paste, 170
    skewered beef with grilled herb polenta, 145
Rotisseries, 48
Rubs:
    ancho chile, 153
    Cajun spice, 120
    chile, 94
    chile-oregano, 118
    chipotle, 112
    five-pepper, 129
    five-spice, 69
    herb and pepper, 87, 107
    lemon-garlic spice, 67
    peppery spice, 102
    pork, Jeff's, 130
    rib, Jeff's, 125, 126
    sage and black pepper, 114
    smoky spice, 138
    Southwest, 150
    spice, 105
    spicy, 72, 88
    sweet hot, 173
Rum:
    and ginger marinade, 117
    and ginger sauce, 196
    mustard, and molasses glaze, 133

S

Safety tips, 53
Sage:
    and black pepper rub, 114
    and garlic paste, 128
Salads:
    jalapeño coleslaw, 155
    pineapple, grilled, and papaya, 90, 91
    potato, Jan's seaside, 155

tomatillo-jícama, 99
Salmon, 65
    smoked, 81
Salsas, 58
    chipotle, 106
    corn, grilled, and tomato, 94
    mango, 118
    mango-mint, 76, *77*
    three-chile, *74, 75*
Salt, 58
Sauces:
    berry coulis, *192, 193*
    chipotle adobo, 119
    garlic, roasted, aïoli, 164
    hamburger goo, spicy, 143
    lime aïoli, 68
    pepper, grilled, and tomato, 95
    pepper, smoke-roasted, coulis, 92–93
    rum and ginger, 196
    see also Barbecue sauce; Glazes; Gravy; Mops; Salsas; Tomato sauce; Vinaigrettes
Scallops, 64
    five-spice, on sweet and sour rice, 69
    miso-crusted, with grilled baby bok choy, 70, 71
Seafood. *See* Fish and seafood
Serrano chiles, 61
Sherry mushroom gravy, 144
Shrimp, 64
    garlic, on grill with lime aïoli, 68
Side dishes:
    grits, garlic-chile, 114, 115
    polenta, herbed, grilled, 145
    tortillas, grilled, 116
    see also Potato(es); Relishes; Rice; Salads; Salsas; Vegetable(s)

Skewer(ed)(s):
  beef, rosemary, with grilled
    herb polenta, 145
  beef and mushroom, with
    sherry mushroom gravy, 144
  lamb, Basque sheep herder's,
    165
  lamb and pepper, with adobo
    rice, 166
  strawberries and bananas with
    berry cream, 195
Slow-roasting, 37–38
Smoke flavor:
  from herbs, 44–45
  from wood, 43–44
Smoker-cookers, offset, 46–47
Smokers, water, 47
Smoky:
  spice rub, 138
  tomato barbecue sauce, 125
Southwest:
  citrus marinade, 99
  rub, 150
Soy-garlic marinade, 70
Spareribs, 127
  slow-cooked, two ways, 126–27
Spit-roasted:
  lamb, boned, stuffed leg of,
    with mint, chile, and
    vinegar mop, 169
  pork loin with sage and garlic
    crust, 128
Squash. *See* Summer squash
Starter fluid, 53
Steaks, 18–19, 21, 135–36
  cuts of, 136
  New York strip or shell, with
    thyme and garlic paste, 140,
    141
  porterhouse, with smoky spice
    rub, 138
  sirloin, chile-bourbon, 139

skirt or flank, with citrus-chile
  marinade, 142
Stovetop grills, 48
Strawberries and bananas,
  skewered, with berry
  cream, 195
Stuffing, mint, oregano, and
  chipotle, 169
Summer squash:
  grilled, with fresh herb
    marinade, 179
  vegetable mixed grill, 180, 181
  zucchini, chèvre, eggplant, and
    roasted pepper pizza, 188
Sweet and sour rice, 69
Sweet hot rub, 173
Swordfish, 65
  steaks with lime-ginger
    pickled onions and papaya
    vinaigrette, 73

T
Tacos, 176
Tarragon:
  and garlic butter, 80
  grilled tomato sauce with red
    peppers and, 182
  lemon paste, 96
Texas-style brisket, 154–55
Thermometers, 49–50
Thyme, 44–45
  and garlic paste, 92, 140
Tomatillo(s), 59
  jícama salad, 99
  vinaigrette, 99
Tomato(es):
  barbecue sauce, smoky, 125
  grilled, 103, 182
  and grilled corn salsa, 94
  mint, and onion relish, 170, 171

smoked, risotto, 96–97
Tomato sauce (with grilled
  tomatoes):
  with basil and garlic, 183
  with chiles, onion, and lime,
    183
  with grilled peppers, 95
  with red peppers and tarragon,
    182
Tortillas, grilled, 116
Tuna, ahi, 65
  with lemon-wasabi marinade
    and mango-mint salsa, 76, 77
Turkey, 85
  roast, with herb and pepper
    rub and smoke-roasted
    yams, 107
  thighs, chipotle, 106

V
Vegetable(s), 175–91
  beans, campfire, 150–51
  bok choy, baby, grilled, 70, 71
  chiles and onions, grilled,
    112–13
  corn, grilled, with chile-garlic
    butter, 191
  eggplant grilled in oregano
    smoke, 178
  green beans, grilled, 86
  greens, bacon-wilted, 88–89
  greens, hot, 123
  mixed grill, 180, 181
  onions, grilled, 88–89, 112–13,
    143
  peppers, grilled, 113
  portobello mushrooms, grilled,
    190
  summer squash, grilled, with
    fresh herb marinade, 179

tomatoes, grilled, 103, 182
yams, smoke-roasted, 107
see also Potato(es)
Vinaigrettes:
  papaya, 73
  tomatillo, 99
Vinegar:
  chile mop, 123
  mint, and chile mop, 169
  mint mop, 173

W
Wasabi, 59
  lemon marinade, 76
  miso marinade, 70
Water smokers, 47
Wine, red, marinade, 165
Woodsmoke, for flavor, 43–44

Y
Yams, smoke-roasted, 107

Z
Zucchini:
  chèvre, eggplant, and roasted
    pepper pizza, 188
  grilled summer squash with
    fresh herb marinade, 179
  vegetable mixed grill, 180, 181

BOOK DESIGN
Susi Oberhelman

PRODUCTION
Kim Tyner

The text in this book was composed in

DANTE
Designed by Ron Carpenter in 1993

ITC FRANKLIN GOTHIC
Designed by Victor Caruso in 1980,
based on original designed by Morris Fuller Benton in 1903

PRINTED AND BOUND IN
Singapore